A
REFUGE
from the
STORM

A
REFUGE
from the
STORM

The Priesthood, the Family, the Church

BOYD K. PACKER

DESERET
BOOK

Salt Lake City, Utah

© 2014 Boyd K. Packer

DESERET BOOK is a registered trademark of Deseret Book Company.

Visit us at DeseretBook.com

Library of Congress Cataloging-in-Publication Data

(CIP data on file)
ISBN 978-1-60907-983-3

Printed in the United States of America
Edwards Brothers Malloy, Ann Arbor, MI

10   9   8   7   6   5   4   3   2   1

CONTENTS

CONTENTS

THE FAMILY

THE CHURCH

And that the gathering together upon
the land of Zion, and upon her stakes, may be
for a defense, and for a refuge from the storm,
and from wrath when it shall be poured out
without mixture upon the whole earth.

DOCTRINE AND COVENANTS 115:6

INTRODUCTION

How does one start a book about the priesthood and the family? You cannot say "in the beginning" because there was not a beginning, and there will be no end. The priesthood is described as the "everlasting priesthood" (Exodus 40:15; Numbers 25:13). It is not an easy thing to expand the mind to try to understand the idea of no beginning and no end. We are governed in life by beginnings and endings—morning and night—and we will not understand the power of the presence of the priesthood until we understand this truth.

The scriptures speak of "from before the foundation of the world" (D&C 124:33, 41; 128:5, 8; 132:5, 63; Moses 5:57) or "from before the world was" (D&C 124:38). Once you place your mind along the way in a continuum, you will be able to see farther ahead and understand farther behind, and the present becomes a treasure of great worth.

The gospel of Jesus Christ enables individuals to become exalted by being part of eternal families. The gospel contains the purpose, the doctrine, and the plan. The priesthood is the power and the authority.

The Church has the means and organization. The exalted, eternal family is the end of the gospel plan. In this book, we will discuss those three interconnected elements of the gospel: the priesthood, the family, and the Church.

The Priesthood

When the priesthood is solidly in place, everything else will fit together. The authority and power of the priesthood form the foundation of all that we do in the Church.

1

WHAT EVERY ELDER—AND SISTER—SHOULD KNOW

A Primer on Principles of Priesthood Government

Less than a year after the Church was organized, the Prophet Joseph Smith received a revelation which said: "Hearken, O ye elders of my church whom I have called, behold I give unto you a commandment, that ye shall assemble yourselves together to agree upon my word; and by the prayer of your faith ye shall receive my law, that ye may know how to govern my church and have all things right before me" (D&C 41:2–3).

There are some things about the priesthood that every member should know if he or she is to understand how the Church is governed to have things right before the Lord. There are principles and precepts and rules which are often overlooked and seldom taught.

Some of these principles are found in the scriptures, others in the handbooks. Some of them are not found in either. They are found in

---

From an address given at a training session of the General Authorities at general conference, April 1992; see *Ensign*, February 1993, 4–13.

the Church. You might call them traditions, but they are more than that. They are revelations which came when the Brethren of the past assembled themselves, agreed upon His word, and offered their prayers of faith.

The Lord then showed them what to do. They received by revelation, "line upon line, precept upon precept," true principles which form the priesthood way of doing things (2 Nephi 28:30; D&C 98:12; see also Isaiah 28:13). These are things we do to have things right before the Lord.

Priesthood is the authority and the power which God has granted to men on earth to act for Him (see JST, Genesis 14:28–31). When we exercise priesthood authority properly, we do what *He* would do if He were present.

The Melchizedek or Higher Priesthood

"There are, in the church, two priesthoods, namely, the Melchizedek and Aaronic, including the Levitical Priesthood. The first is called the Melchizedek Priesthood because Melchizedek was such a great high priest. Before his day it was called *the Holy Priesthood, after the Order of the Son of God*" (D&C 107:1–3).

The Melchizedek Priesthood is also spoken of in the scriptures as the "greater priesthood" or the priesthood "which is after the holiest order of God" (D&C 84:18–19) and the priesthood "after the order of mine Only Begotten Son (D&C 124:123; see also D&C 76:57).

"Out of respect or reverence to the name of the Supreme Being, to avoid the too frequent repetition of his name, they, the church, in ancient days, called that priesthood after Melchizedek, or the Melchizedek Priesthood" (D&C 107:4). We can understand why that should be. The name of the priesthood is frequently talked about in meetings and lessons and is printed in handbooks and manuals. It would be irreverent to use informally the sacred title which includes the name of Deity.

Melchizedek, the great high priest, is identified in the scriptures

4

as the "king of Salem" or, as we would say today, Jerusalem (Genesis 14:18; Alma 13:17–18). "And it was this same Melchizedek to whom Abraham paid tithes" (Alma 13:15; see also Genesis 14:20).

There are references to a patriarchal priesthood. The patriarchal order is not a third, separate priesthood (see D&C 84:6–17; 107:40–57). Whatever relates to the patriarchal order is embraced in the Melchizedek Priesthood. "All other authorities and offices in the church are appendages to [the Melchizedek] priesthood" (D&C 107:5). The patriarchal order is a part of the Melchizedek Priesthood which enables endowed and worthy men to preside over their posterity in time and eternity.

The Aaronic or Lesser Priesthood

"The second priesthood is called the Priesthood of Aaron, because it was conferred upon Aaron and his seed. . . . It is called the lesser priesthood . . . because it is an appendage to the greater, or the Melchizedek Priesthood, and has power in administering outward ordinances" (D&C 107:13–14).

It is sometimes called the preparatory priesthood because it prepares one for the higher priesthood.

The Levitical Priesthood (see Hebrews 7:11; D&C 107:6, 10) is an order in or a part of the Aaronic Priesthood. Moses and Aaron belonged to the tribe of Levi (see Exodus 2:1–2, 10; 4:14). During the exodus from Egypt, the Levites were given priestly responsibilities concerning the tabernacle and always camped nearest to it (see Numbers 3:5–39). While the Levitical order does not function today, its privileges and authority are embraced within the Aaronic Priesthood for whatever future use the Lord may direct.

The Keys of the Priesthood

There are keys of the priesthood. While the word *key* has other meanings, like keys of wisdom or keys of knowledge, the keys of the priesthood are the right to preside and direct the affairs of the Church within a jurisdiction. All priesthood keys are within The Church of Jesus Christ of Latter-day Saints, and no keys exist outside the Church on earth.

All men who are ordained Apostles and sustained as members of the Quorum of Twelve Apostles have all priesthood keys conferred upon them (see D&C 27:13; 110:11–16; 112:30).

The President of the Church is the only person on earth who has the right to exercise all the keys in their fulness (see D&C 132:7). He receives this authority by setting apart by the Twelve Apostles.

"The power and authority of the higher, or Melchizedek Priesthood, is to hold the keys of all the spiritual blessings of the church. . . .

"The power and authority of the lesser, or Aaronic Priesthood, is to hold the keys of the ministering of angels, and to administer in outward ordinances, the letter of the gospel, the baptism of repentance for the remission of sins, agreeable to the covenants and commandments" (D&C 107:18, 20).

Keys are conferred upon a man when he is set apart to be a president of a stake or a quorum, or as a bishop. Counselors do not receive keys.

The Priesthood Is Not Divisible

The priesthood is greater than any of its offices. When someone first receives the Aaronic or Melchizedek Priesthood, it is conferred upon him by the laying on of hands. After the priesthood has been conferred upon him, he is ordained to an office in the priesthood. All offices derive their authority from the priesthood.

The priesthood is not divisible. An elder holds as much priesthood as an Apostle (see D&C 20:38). When a man receives the priesthood, he receives all of it. However, there are offices within the priesthood—divisions of authority and responsibility. One may exercise his priesthood according to the rights of the office to which he is ordained or set apart.

"The Melchizedek Priesthood holds the right of presidency, and has power and authority over all the offices in the church in all ages of the world, to administer in spiritual things" (D&C 107:8).

Whoever holds the Melchizedek Priesthood or higher priesthood holds all of the authority of the Aaronic or lesser priesthood as well.

Ordained Offices

The ordained offices in the Aaronic Priesthood are:

> Deacon
> Teacher
> Priest

The bishop is the president of the Aaronic Priesthood. He has the keys conferred upon him at the time of his ordination. He delegates responsibility to his counselors. The three of them form the bishopric, which is a presidency (D&C 107:15–17).

The ordained offices in the Melchizedek Priesthood are:

> Elder
> High Priest
> Patriarch
> Seventy
> Apostle

Besides identifying a specific ordained office in the Melchizedek Priesthood, the title "elder" is used to identify anyone holding the higher priesthood. Therefore Seventies and Apostles may be referred to as "elder" (D&C 20:38).

While all who have had the Melchizedek Priesthood conferred upon them receive the full priesthood, sometimes one office is spoken of as being "higher than" or "lower than" another office. Rather than "higher" or "lower," offices in the Melchizedek Priesthood represent different areas of service.

There are different rights, privileges, and authorities which expand with each succeeding office. For instance, the offices of teacher or priest are spoken of as being higher than the office of deacon. A priest in the Aaronic Priesthood can perform any duty assigned to the teachers or deacons. For example, a priest may pass the sacrament, a duty usually assigned to deacons. A deacon, on the other hand, cannot bless the sacrament nor perform baptisms, duties which are assigned to priests.

An elder can perform any duty assigned to any office in the Aaronic Priesthood, but he cannot do some things which belong to the office of high priest. These principles of priesthood government are established by revelation and do not change.

Quorums

In the dispensation of the fulness of times, the Lord has instructed that the priesthood should be organized into quorums, meaning selected assemblies of brethren given authority that His business might be transacted and His work proceed.

A quorum is a brotherhood. Except for the offices of bishop and patriarch, those ordained to offices in the priesthood are organized into quorums.

Though one may be called to and released from ecclesiastical assignments for which one is set apart, membership in a quorum is a steady, sustaining citizenship. It becomes a right of one ordained to an office in the priesthood. And the holding of the priesthood, including the attendant membership in the quorum, is to be regarded as a sacred privilege.

Melchizedek Priesthood quorums are:

> The First Presidency
> The Quorum of the Twelve
> Seventies quorums

High priests quorums

Elders quorums

Aaronic Priesthood quorums are:

Priests quorums

Teachers quorums

Deacons quorums

Each quorum is presided over by a president or a presidency. The Quorum of the Twelve is presided over by one president, the President of the Twelve (see D&C 124:127), as is the priests quorum presided over by the bishop (see D&C 107:87).

The Seventies quorums are presided over by seven presidents (see D&C 107:93). All other quorums are presided over by a presidency consisting of a president, a first counselor, and a second counselor.

The Oath and Covenant of the Priesthood

There is an oath and covenant of the priesthood. The covenant part rests with man; the oath with God. The Melchizedek Priesthood is received by covenant. A man's covenant with God is: to be faithful and magnify his callings in the priesthood; to give heed to the words of eternal life; and to live by every word that proceeds forth from the mouth of God (see D&C 84:33, 43, 44).

God, for His part, declares with an everlasting oath that all who receive the priesthood and obey the covenants that pertain to that priesthood shall receive "all that [the] Father hath" (D&C 84:38).

"And this is according to the oath and covenant which belongeth to the priesthood.

"Therefore, all those who receive the priesthood, receive this oath and covenant of my Father, which he cannot break, neither can it be moved" (D&C 84:39–40).

Ordination and Setting Apart

There are two ways authority is conferred in the Church: by *ordination* and by *setting apart*. Offices in the priesthood—deacon, teacher, priest, elder, high priest, patriarch, seventy, and Apostle—always come by ordination. The keys of presidency and the authority to act in callings in the priesthood are received by setting apart.

For instance, the office of elder in the Melchizedek Priesthood is an ordained office, but the office of president of an elders quorum is an office to which one is set apart rather than ordained. In either case, he is given a blessing to accompany his service in an office to which he is ordained or set apart.

There are many "set apart" offices in the Church in both the priesthood and the auxiliary organizations. Some duties are inherent in the priesthood and one need not be set apart to do them. Visiting the homes of members (home teaching) is an example.

Because women are not ordained to the priesthood, when sisters are set apart to offices, including the office of president in an auxiliary, they receive authority, responsibility, and blessings connected with the office, but they do not receive keys.

Limits to Authority

Ordinarily, the privileges connected with an ordination to the priesthood may be exercised anywhere in the Church. Priesthood holders need no prior authorization to perform ordinances or blessings that are not recorded on the records of the Church, such as consecrating oil, administering to the sick, and giving fathers' blessings.

The priesthood is always regulated by those who have the keys, and ordinances must be authorized by the presiding authority who holds the proper keys and priesthood if the ordinance is to be recorded on the records of the Church.

Authority connected to an office to which one is set apart has limits, including geographic ones. The authority of a man set apart as president of a stake is limited to the boundaries of that stake. He is not a stake president to members in a neighboring stake, nor is a bishop the bishop over members outside his ward. When a man is ordained a bishop, he is also set apart to preside in a specific ward and has no authority outside its boundaries. When he is released as bishop of that ward, he may still hold the ordained office of bishop, but he cannot function unless he is set apart again to preside over a ward.

When a patriarch is ordained, he is set apart to give blessings to members of his own stake or to those who come into the boundaries of his stake with a recommend from proper authority from a stake where there is no patriarch. These principles of priesthood government are established by revelations.

Usual Age at the Time of Call to Priesthood Offices

So that there may be order in advancement in the priesthood, a minimum age is set for receiving the priesthood and for ordination to each succeeding office within the priesthood.

The Aaronic Priesthood is conferred upon a young man when he is ordained a deacon at age twelve or older. He then joins a quorum of up to twelve deacons (see D&C 107:85). When he is fourteen, he may be ordained to the office of teacher. He then joins a quorum of up to twenty-four teachers (see D&C 107:86). When he is sixteen, he may be ordained a priest. He then joins a quorum of up to forty-eight priests (see D&C 107:87). When he is eighteen or older, he may have the Melchizedek Priesthood conferred upon him and be ordained an elder. He then joins a quorum of up to ninety-six elders.

The revelations state that "the duty of the president over the office of elders is to preside over ninety-six elders, and to sit in council with them, and to teach them according to the covenants" (D&C 107:89). The high priests have no specific age and there is no specific number in a high priests quorum. High priests are organized into groups with group leaders. The stake presidency is the presidency of the high priests quorum in the stake.

Calls to Office

In the Church we do not assume authority belonging to either an ordained or a set apart office or calling. We must be called to a position and sustained, be ordained or set apart, and be given authority. The fifth article of faith says, "We believe that a man must be called of God, by prophecy, and by the laying on of hands by those who are in authority, to preach the Gospel and administer in the ordinances thereof."

Every elder should know that a call is more than an invitation or a request, even more than an assignment. Too frequently we hear such expressions as, "I have been asked to serve as a counselor in the elders quorum presidency." It would be more proper to say, "I have been *called* to serve as a counselor."

We do not call ourselves to offices in the Church. Rather, we respond to the call of those who preside over us. It is the responsibility of those who preside to prayerfully consult the Lord as to His will concerning a position in the Church. Then the principle of revelation is at work. The call is then delivered by the presiding officer, who is acting for the Lord.

We do not, under ordinary circumstances, refuse a call. Neither do we ask for a release beyond calling to the attention of the presiding officer circumstances which may make a release advisable.

When we refer to those who have been called to a presiding position by the title of their office, such as bishop or president, it lends dignity to the office and reminds the one holding it of his sacred responsibility, and it reminds us of our obligation to follow their counsel and respond to their calls.

Sustaining in an Office

The Aaronic or Melchizedek Priesthood is not conferred, nor is one ordained or set apart to an office in either priesthood, unless he is willing to live the standards of worthiness. Those standards include moral purity, the payment of tithes, keeping the Word of Wisdom, and general standards of Christian conduct.

He must be called by those who have the proper authority; sustained, or voted on, in an appropriate meeting; and ordained or set apart by one who has the authority. This is called "common consent" or the voice of the people (see D&C 41:9). This follows the instructions given in revelation:

"Again I say unto you, that it shall not be given to any one to go forth to preach my gospel, or to build up my church, except he be ordained by some one who has authority, and it is known to the church that he has authority and has been regularly ordained by the heads of the church" (D&C 42:11).

Notice that there are two requirements: First, we must receive authority from someone who has it and has been ordained by the heads of the Church. Next, it must be known in the Church that he has the authority. The sustaining in the priesthood and the setting apart to office is done openly where it can be known to the Church who has authority, as the scriptures require.

There is great safety to the Church in having the names of those called to offices in the Church presented in the proper meeting (see D&C 20:65). Anyone who is a pretender or a deceiver will be recognized. If someone claims to have been secretly ordained to a special calling or higher order of priesthood, you may know immediately that the claim is false!

The names of those to be ordained to the Melchizedek Priesthood or to another office in the Melchizedek Priesthood are presented in stake or district conferences. (A district in a mission is like a stake. A branch in a stake or district is like a ward.) The congregation is asked to approve the ordination by raising the right hand, or, if opposed to the ordination, they may signify by the same sign. This occurs in a stake meeting because the stake presidency presides over the Melchizedek Priesthood.

In an emergency—for instance, if a young man is leaving for a mission and has not been ordained an elder—the stake presidency should have his name presented for sustaining in his own ward sacrament meeting. The ordination is then presented for ratification at the first appropriate stake meeting. Only in an emergency would this process be followed; otherwise it is not in order.

Advancements in the Aaronic Priesthood are sustained in ward meetings because the bishopric presides over the Aaronic Priesthood. Members called to positions in the auxiliary organizations are also sustained before being set apart in the appropriate stake or ward meeting.

The bishop, as the common judge, presides over all members of his ward, including holders of the Melchizedek Priesthood (see D&C 107:74). All members pay tithing to the bishop and should seek counsel from him.

The bishop must be a high priest (see D&C 68:19; 84:29, 107:17, 69–73) and is designated as the presiding high priest in the ward. In this capacity he may preside over the ward council and ward priesthood executive council meetings, where elders quorum and high priests group officers are in attendance.

While the bishop may recommend that a man be ordained an elder or high priest, and verify his worthiness, the approval and ordination are under the direction of the stake presidency. A bishop does not call nor can he release the presidency of an elders quorum; they come under the direction of the stake presidency.

A bishop might convene a disciplinary council to consider the transgression of an elder in his ward. He may disfellowship the elder if that is merited, but he cannot deprive him of his priesthood by excommunication. That would require a disciplinary council presided over by the stake presidency, who govern the Melchizedek Priesthood.

Temple Recommends

The bishop has authority to judge the worthiness of a member to receive a temple recommend, and his counselors have the authority to assist in interviewing ward members for subsequent temple recommends. The stake president or his counselors also interview those going to the temple because there members will participate in ordinances of the Melchizedek Priesthood.

More Than One Ordained Office

Sometimes a man may hold more than one ordained office at a time. For instance, both bishops and patriarchs are also high priests. Also, a man may hold an ordained office and be set apart to other offices. For instance, an ordained elder may be set apart to offices such as president of his quorum, ward mission leader, or Sunday School president.

Let Every Man Act in the Office to Which He Is Called

The Lord counseled us to "let every man learn his duty, and to act in the office in which he is appointed, in all diligence" (D&C 107:99). An elder who has been called to an office of presidency should respect the callings of those over whom he presides. He should let, indeed help, them do that which they are called to do without usurping their responsibilities.

In turn, holders of the priesthood should avoid going around their file leader to a higher authority supposing that they will receive better counsel or more wisdom, spirituality, or authority. It is better to respect the callings of those over whom we preside and of those who preside over us.

The Name of the Lord

Rather than using the term "Mormon Church," we should call the Church by its name—The Church of Jesus Christ of Latter-day Saints, "for thus," the Lord told us in a revelation, "shall my church be called in the last days" (D&C 115:3–4).

When we officiate in the priesthood, we always do it in the name of the Lord (see 3 Nephi 27:1–10). When we act according to the proper order of things, we act for the Lord, and it is as though He were there insofar as the validity of the ordinance is concerned. The Lord said to one man who was being set apart to preach the gospel: "I will lay my hand upon you *by the hand of my servant Sidney Rigdon,* and you shall receive my Spirit, the Holy Ghost, even the Comforter, which shall teach you the peaceable things of the kingdom" (D&C 36:2; emphasis added).

Exceptions

Sometimes there must be exceptions to the rules and principles by which the priesthood is governed. Care must be taken to see that all things having to do with ordinations and settings apart are done in proper order. Generally, exceptions are approved by the First Presidency of the Church.

Recording Ordinations and Settings Apart

Proper records are always made of ordinations and settings apart in the Church (see D&C 20:63–64; 85:1–2; 127:9). For "behold, mine house is a house of order, saith the Lord God, and not a house of confusion" (D&C 132:8; see also D&C 88:119; 109:8).

The Power of Godliness

The Melchizedek Priesthood "administereth the gospel and holdeth the key of the mysteries of the kingdom, even the key of the knowledge of God.

"Therefore, in the ordinances thereof, the power of godliness is manifest.

"And without the ordinances thereof, and the authority of the priesthood, the power of godliness is not manifest unto men in the flesh;

"For without this no man can see the face of God . . . and live" (D&C 84:19–22).

The priesthood, which is always associated with God's work, "continueth in the church of God in all generations, and is without beginning of days or end of years" (D&C 87:17).

"For whoso is faithful unto the obtaining these two priesthoods of which I have spoken, and the magnifying their calling, are sanctified by the spirit unto the renewing of their bodies.

"They become the sons of Moses and of Aaron and the seed of Abraham, and the church and kingdom, and the elect of God.

"And also all they who receive this priesthood receive me, saith the Lord;

"For he that receiveth my servants receiveth me;

"And he that receiveth me receiveth my Father;

"And he that receiveth my Father receiveth my Father's kingdom; therefore all that my Father hath shall be given unto him" (D&C 84:33–38).

2

THE POWER OF
THE PRIESTHOOD

Years ago we began correlation under the direction of President Harold B. Lee. At that time, President Thomas S. Monson said: "Today, we are encamped against the greatest array of sin, vice, and evil ever assembled before our eyes. . . . The battle plan whereby we fight to save the souls of men is not our own. It [came through] the inspiration and revelation of the Lord" ("Correlation Brings Blessings," *Relief Society Magazine,* Apr. 1967, 247).

During those years of correlation, the whole operating face of the Church was changed. The entire curriculum was restructured. The objectives and relationships of the organizations one to another were redefined. The key word during those years of correlation and restructuring was *priesthood.*

President Monson also spoke of Gideon, a hero in the Old Testament. Gideon was chosen to lead the armies of Israel, thousands strong. But of them all, he chose only three hundred men.

From an address given at general conference, April 3, 2010; see *Ensign,* May 2010, 6–10.

Gideon had an interesting way of selecting his recruits. When the men drank water at a stream, most "bowed down . . . to drink." Those he passed over. A few scooped up water in their hands and drank, remaining completely alert. They were the ones chosen (see Judges 7:4–8).

We live in a day of "wars [and] rumors of wars, and earthquakes in divers places" (Mormon 8:30). As prophesied, "the whole earth [is] in commotion" (D&C 45:26) and "Satan is abroad in the land" (D&C 52:14). He seeks to destroy all that is good and righteous (see D&C 10:22–23). He is Lucifer, who was cast out of the presence of God (see Revelation 12:7–9). Against all of that, we have very positive feelings about what lies ahead.

Gideon's small force succeeded because, as the record states, "they stood every man in his place" (Judges 7:21).

This "dispensation of the fulness of times" (D&C 112:30) opened with the appearance of the Father and the Son to the boy Joseph Smith (see Joseph Smith—History 1:17). Next the angel Moroni showed Joseph where the plates containing the Book of Mormon had been buried (see Joseph Smith—History 1:33–34, 59). Joseph was given power to translate them (see Book of Mormon introduction).

During translation Joseph and Oliver Cowdery read about baptism. They prayed to know what to do (see Joseph Smith—History 1:68–69). There appeared to them an angelic messenger, John the Baptist. He conferred upon them the Aaronic Priesthood, "which holds the keys of the ministering of angels, and of the gospel of repentance, and of baptism by immersion for the remission of sins" (D&C 13:1).

The Apostles Peter, James, and John, who were closest to the Lord in His ministry, appeared next and conferred upon Joseph and Oliver the higher priesthood (see D&C 27:12–13), or "the Holy Priesthood, after the Order of the Son of God" (D&C 107:3). The priesthood, the scriptures direct, was to be named after Melchizedek, the great high priest to whom Abraham paid tithes (see D&C 107:2–4).

This then became their authority. Through the keys of the priest-hood, they had access to all of the powers of heaven. They were com-manded to carry the gospel unto all nations (see D&C 42:58).

It has never been easy to live the gospel of Jesus Christ. It was not easy when He lived, and it was not easy in the early days of the Church. The early Saints were subjected to unspeakable suffering and opposition.

It has been over 180 years since the priesthood was restored. We now number nearly fifteen million members. Even so, we are a tiny fraction when compared to the billions of people on earth. But we are who we are, and we know what we know, and we are to go forth and preach the gospel.

The Book of Mormon makes it clear that we never will dominate by numbers. But we have the power of the priesthood (see 1 Nephi 14:14).

The prophet Nephi wrote, "It came to pass that I beheld the church of the Lamb of God, and its numbers were few . . . ; neverthe-less, I beheld that the church of the Lamb, who were the saints of God, were also upon all the face of the earth; and their dominions upon the face of the earth were small" (1 Nephi 14:12).

President Joseph Fielding Smith said, "While it may be said . . . that we are but a handful in comparison with . . . the world, yet we may be compared with the leaven of which the Savior spoke, which will eventually leaven [or lift] the whole world" (in Conference Report, Oct. 1968, 123).

We can and in due time certainly will influence all of humanity. It will be known who we are and why we are. It might seem hopeless; it is monumentally difficult; but it is not only possible but certain that we will win the battle against Satan.

It is crucial for everyone—men and women alike—to understand what is expected of the brethren who hold the priesthood. Unless we enlist the attention of the mothers and daughters and sisters—who have influence on their husbands, fathers, sons, and brothers—we cannot progress. The priesthood will lose great power if the sisters are neglected.

Priesthood is the authority and the power which God has granted to men on earth to act for Him (see *Teachings of Presidents of the Church: Joseph F. Smith* [1998], 141). When priesthood authority is exercised properly, priesthood bearers do what He would do if He were present.

We have done very well at distributing the *authority* of the priesthood. We have priesthood authority planted nearly everywhere. We have quorums of elders and high priests worldwide. But distributing the *authority* of the priesthood has raced, I think, ahead of distributing the *power* of the priesthood. The priesthood does not have the strength that it should have and will not have until the *power* of the priesthood is firmly fixed in the families as it should be.

President Harold B. Lee stated: "It seems clear to me that the Church has *no choice*—and never has had—but to do more to assist the *family* in carrying out *its* divine mission, not only because that is the order of heaven, but also because that is the most *practical* contribution we can make to our youth—to help improve the quality of life in the Latter-day Saint homes. As important as our many programs and organizational efforts are, these *should not* supplant the home; they should *support* the home" ("Preparing Our Youth," *Ensign,* Mar. 1971, 3; emphasis added).

President Joseph F. Smith made this statement about the priesthood in the home: "In the home the presiding authority is always vested in the father, and in all home affairs and family matters there is no other authority paramount. To illustrate this principle, a single incident will perhaps suffice. It sometimes happens that the elders are called in to administer to the members of a family. Among these elders there may be presidents of stakes, apostles, or even members of the First Presidency of the Church. It is not proper under these circumstances

21

for the father to stand back and expect the elders to direct the administration of this important ordinance. The father is there. It is his right and it is his duty to preside. He should select the one who is to administer the oil, and the one who is to be mouth in prayer, and he should not feel that because there are present presiding authorities in the Church that he is therefore divested of his rights to direct the administration of that blessing of the gospel in his home. (If the father be absent, the mother should request the presiding authority present to take charge.) The father presides at the table, at prayer, and gives general directions relating to his family life whoever may be present" (*Gospel Doctrine*, 5th ed. [1939], 287).

During the Vietnam War, we held a series of special meetings for members of the Church called into military service. After such a meeting in Chicago, I was standing next to President Harold B. Lee when a fine young Latter-day Saint told President Lee that he was on leave to visit his home and then had orders to Vietnam. He asked President Lee to give him a blessing.

Much to my surprise, President Lee said, "Your father should give you the blessing."

Very disappointed, the boy said, "My father wouldn't know how to give a blessing."

President Lee answered, "Go home, my boy, and tell your father that you are going away to war and want to receive a father's blessing from him. If he does not know how, tell him that you will sit on a chair. He can stand behind you and put his hands on your head and say whatever comes."

This young soldier went away sorrowing.

About two years later I met him again. I do not recall where. He reminded me of that experience and said, "I did as I was told to do. I explained to my father that I would sit on the chair and that he should put his hands on my head. The power of the priesthood filled both

22

of us. That was a strength and protection in those perilous months of battle."

Another time I was in a distant city. After a conference we were ordaining and setting apart leaders. As we concluded, the stake president asked, "Can we ordain a young man to be an elder who is leaving for the mission field?" The answer, of course, was yes.

As the young man came forward, he motioned for three brethren to follow and stand in for his ordination.

I noticed on the back row a carbon copy of this boy, and I asked, "Is that your father?"

The young man said, "Yes."

I said, "Your father will ordain you."

And he protested, "But I've already asked another brother to ordain me."

And I said, "Young man, your father will ordain you, and you'll live to thank the Lord for this day."

Then the father came forward.

Thank goodness he was an elder. Had he not been, he soon could have been! In the military they would call that a battlefield commission. Sometimes such things are done in the Church.

The father did not know how to ordain his son. I put my arm around him and coached him through the ordinance. When he was finished, the young man was an elder.

Then something wonderful happened. Completely changed, the father and son embraced. It was obvious that had never happened before.

The father, through his tears, said, "I didn't get to ordain my other boys."

Think how much more was accomplished than if another had ordained him, even an Apostle.

While the priesthood is presently all over the world, we call on every elder and high priest, every holder of the priesthood to stand, like

Gideon's small but powerful force of three hundred, *in his own place.* We now must awaken in every elder and high priest, in every quorum and group, and in the father of every home the power of the priesthood of the Almighty.

The Lord said that "the weak things of the world shall come forth and break down the mighty and strong ones" (D&C 1:19).

The prophet Nephi also told of "the power of the Lamb of God, that it descended upon the saints of the church of the Lamb, and upon the covenant people of the Lord, who were scattered upon all the face of the earth" and said that "they were armed with righteousness and with the power of God in great glory" (1 Nephi 14:14).

We need everyone. The tired or worn out or lazy and even those who are bound down with guilt must be restored through repentance and forgiveness. Too many of our priesthood brethren are living below their privileges and the Lord's expectations.

We must go forward, confident of the supernal power of the priesthood. It is a source of strength and encouragement to know who we are and what we have and what we must do in the work of the Almighty.

The Lord has said, "I, the Lord, am bound when ye do what I say; but when ye do not what I say, ye have no promise" (D&C 82:10).

Homes without priesthood holders are to be watched over and ministered to by the quorums of the priesthood. In this manner no blessings will be found wanting in any dwelling within the Church.

Years ago a family gathered at the bedside of an aged little Danish woman. Among them was her middle-aged, wayward son. For the past number of years he had been living at home.

Tearfully he pleaded, "Mama, you've got to live. Mama, you can't die." He said, "Mama, you can't go. I won't let you go."

The little mother looked up at her son and in her broken Danish accent said, "But ver is yo powah?"—where is your power?

Paul said:

"[We] are built upon the foundation of the apostles and prophets, Jesus Christ himself being the chief corner stone;

"In whom all the building fitly framed together groweth unto an holy temple in the Lord:

"In whom ye also are builded together for an habitation of God through the Spirit" (Ephesians 2:20–22).

That the work of the Lord will prevail is not a question. That we must marshal all of our efforts and unify ourselves are givens.

The authority of the priesthood is with us. After all that we have correlated and organized, it is now our responsibility to activate the *power* of the priesthood in the Church. *Authority* in the priesthood comes by way of ordination; *power* in the priesthood comes through faithful and obedient living in honoring covenants. It is increased by exercising and using the priesthood in righteousness.

Now, if you are a father, I would remind you of the sacred nature of your calling. You have the power of the priesthood directly from the Lord to protect your home. There will be times when all that stands as a shield between your family and the adversary's mischief will be that power. You will receive direction from the Lord by way of the gift of the Holy Ghost.

The adversary is not actively disturbing our Church meetings—perhaps only occasionally. By and large we are free to assemble as we wish without much disruption. But he and those who follow him are persistent in attacking the home and the family.

The ultimate end of all activity in the Church is that a man and his wife and their children might be happy at home, protected by the principles and laws of the gospel, sealed safely in the covenants of the everlasting priesthood.

Every law and principle and power, every belief, every ordinance and ordination, every covenant, every sermon and every sacrament, every counsel and correction, the sealings, the calls, the releases, the service—all these have as their ultimate purpose the perfection of the individual and the family, for the Lord has said, "This is my work and my glory—to bring to pass the immortality and eternal life of man" (Moses 1:39).

I bear witness of the power of the priesthood given to the Church to protect us and guide us. And because we have that, we have no fear of the future. Fear is the opposite of faith. We move forward, certain that the Lord will watch over us, particularly in the family.

3

THE TWELVE APOSTLES

Jesus Calls the Twelve Apostles

In the course of organizing His Church, Jesus "went out into a mountain to pray, and continued all night in prayer to God. And when it was day, he called unto him his disciples: and of them he chose twelve, whom also he named apostles" (Luke 6:12–13). They were called from the ordinary paths of life.

Peter was the first called, and the Lord said to him, "I will give unto thee the keys of the kingdom of heaven: and whatsoever thou shalt bind on earth shall be bound in heaven: and whatsoever thou shalt loose on earth shall be loosed in heaven" (Matthew 16:19). This same sacred authority is inherent in the ordination of every Apostle.

Paul taught that the apostles and prophets were called "for the perfecting of the saints, for the work of the ministry, for the edifying of the body of Christ," and he declared that these offices would endure

From an address given at general conference, October 5, 1996; see *Ensign,* Nov. 1996, 6–8.

"till we all come in the unity of the faith, and of the knowledge of the Son of God" (Ephesians 4:12–13).

The Apostasy and the Restoration

The Apostles in time were gone and, with them, the keys. Paul had prophesied of men being "carried about with every wind of doctrine" (Ephesians 4:14). And so it was; instead of unity of faith, there came division and disunity.

It was in this circumstance that young Joseph Smith prayed to know which of all the churches was true and which he should join.

Joseph's vision of the Father and the Son opened this dispensation. Then came the restoration of the fulness of the gospel of Jesus Christ with the same organization that existed in the primitive Church, built upon the foundation of apostles and prophets (see Articles of Faith 1:6; Ephesians 2:20).

Some suppose that the organization was handed to the Prophet Joseph Smith like a set of plans and specifications for a building, with all of the details known at the beginning. But it did not come that way. Rather, it came a piece at a time as the Brethren were ready and as they inquired of God.

The Melchizedek Priesthood, the consummate authority given to man from God, was restored under the hands of Peter, James, and John. By them, the Lord said:

"I have ordained you and confirmed you to be apostles, and especial witnesses of my name, and bear the keys of your ministry and of the same things which I revealed unto them;

"Unto whom I have committed the keys of my kingdom, and a dispensation of the gospel for the last times" (D&C 27:12–13).

The First Presidency was in place by 1833; then two years later, in February of 1835, came the Quorum of the Twelve Apostles. And that is as it should be. The First Presidency came first in sequence and stands first in authority. And true to the pattern, it was made of men called from the ordinary pursuits of life.

Apostles Are Prophets, Seers, and Revelators

With the First Presidency and the Quorum of the Twelve in place, with the offices of the Seventy and the Presiding Bishopric revealed, the proper order of things prevails. But there is a difference. Perhaps President J. Reuben Clark Jr. said it best:

"Some of the General Authorities [the Apostles] have had assigned to them a special calling; they possess a special gift; they are sustained as prophets, seers, and revelators, which gives them a special spiritual endowment in connection with their teaching of [this] people. They have the right, the power, and the authority to declare the mind and will of God to his people, subject to the overall power and authority of the President of the Church. Others of the General Authorities are not given this special spiritual endowment . . . ; the resulting limitation . . . applies to every other officer and member of the Church, for none of them is spiritually endowed as a prophet, seer, and revelator" ("When Are Church Leaders' Words Entitled to Claim of Scripture?" *Church News*, 31 July 1954, 9–10).

Furthermore, President Clark said that among those of the Twelve and the Presidency, "only the President of the Church, the Presiding High Priest, is sustained as Prophet, Seer, and Revelator for the Church, and he alone has the right to receive revelations for the Church, either new or amendatory, or to give authoritative interpretations of scriptures that shall be binding on the Church, or change in any way the existing doctrines of the Church" (Ibid., 10).

It took a generation of asking and receiving before the order of things as we know it today was firmly in place. Each move to perfect that order has come about in response to a need and in answer to prayer. And that process continues in our day.

The Ministry of the Twelve

"The Twelve are a Traveling Presiding High Council, to officiate in the name of the Lord, under the direction of the Presidency of the Church, agreeable to the institution of heaven; to build up the church, and regulate all the affairs of the same in all nations" (D&C 107:33).

Where the First Presidency cannot go, the Twelve are sent "to unlock the door of the kingdom in all places" (D&C 112:17; see also D&C 107:35; 124:128). They are commissioned to go to all the world, for the word *apostle* means "one [who is] sent forth" (Bible Dictionary, "Apostle," 612).

"Wherefore," the Lord said, "in whatsoever place ye shall proclaim my name an effectual door shall be opened unto you, that they may receive my word" (D&C 112:19). And He promised, "Be thou humble; and the Lord thy God shall lead thee by the hand, and give thee answer to thy prayers" (D&C 112:10).

The Twelve Apostles "are called to be . . . special witnesses of the name of Christ in all the world" (D&C 107:23). Each carries that certain witness that Jesus is the Christ. President Joseph Fielding Smith taught that "every member of the Church should have the impressions on his soul made by the Holy Ghost that Jesus is the Son of God indelibly pictured so that they cannot be forgotten" ("The Twelve Apostles" [address to seminary and institute faculty, 18 June 1958], 6).

From Nephi we know that "angels speak by the power of the Holy Ghost" (2 Nephi 32:3). Mormon told us that "the office of their ministry is to call men unto repentance, and to fulfil and to do the work of the covenants of the Father, which he hath made unto the children of men, to prepare the way among the children of men." Mormon further explained that angels accomplish their ministry "by declaring the word of Christ unto the chosen vessels of the Lord, that they may bear testimony of him. And by so doing, the Lord God prepareth the way that the residue of men may have faith in Christ, that the Holy Ghost may have place in their hearts, according to the power thereof; and after this manner bringeth to pass the Father, the covenants which he hath made unto the children of men" (Moroni 7:31–32).

Apostles Have the Gift of Discernment

There is a power of discernment granted "unto such as God shall appoint . . . to watch over [his] church" (D&C 46:27). To discern means "to see."

President Harold B. Lee told me once of a conversation he had with Elder Charles A. Callis of the Quorum of the Twelve. Elder Callis had remarked that the gift of discernment was an awesome burden to carry. To see clearly what is ahead and yet find members slow to respond or resistant to counsel or even rejecting the witness of the apostles and prophets brings deep sorrow.

Nevertheless, "the responsibility of leading this church" must rest upon us until "you shall appoint others to succeed you" (Declaration of the Twelve Apostles, reporting March 1844 meeting of the Twelve, Brigham Young Papers, Church History Library).

Warning to Wrongful Critics

The Lord warned us of those few in the Church "who have professed to know my name and have not known me, and have blasphemed against me in the midst of my house" (D&C 112:26).

"Thy voice," the Lord commanded the Twelve, "shall be a rebuke unto the transgressor; and at thy rebuke let the tongue of the slanderer cease its perverseness" (D&C 112:9).

Some few within the Church openly—or perhaps far worse, in the darkness of anonymity—reproach their leaders in the wards and stakes and in the Church, seeking to make them "an offender for a word" (Isaiah 29:21; see also 2 Nephi 27:32), as Isaiah said. To them the Lord said:

"Cursed are all those that shall lift up the heel against mine anointed, saith the Lord, and cry they have sinned when they have not sinned . . . but have done that which was meet in mine eyes, and which I commanded them.

"But those who cry transgression do it because they are the servants of sin, and are the children of disobedience themselves. . . .

" . . . Because they have offended my little ones they shall be severed from the ordinances of mine house.

"Their basket shall not be full, their houses and their barns shall perish, and they themselves shall be despised by those that flattered them.

"They shall not have right to the priesthood, nor their posterity after them from generation to generation" (D&C 121:16–17, 19–21).

That terrible penalty will not apply to those who try as best they can to live the gospel and sustain their leaders. Nor need it apply to those who in the past have been guilty of indifference or even opposition if they will repent, confess their transgressions, and forsake them (see D&C 58:43).

Unity of First Presidency and Twelve

President Gordon B. Hinckley on occasion reminded the Brethren that, while we are men called from the ordinary pursuits of life, there rests upon us a sacred ministry. And we take comfort in what the Lord said to the original Twelve: "Ye have not chosen me, but I have chosen you, and ordained you" (John 15:16).

While each feels his own limitation, there is strength in unity. Never in the history of the Church have the Brethren of the First Presidency and the Twelve been more united.

Each week we meet together in the temple. We open the meeting by kneeling in prayer, and we close with prayer. Every prayer is offered in the spirit of submission and obedience to Him who called us and whose servants and witnesses we are.

The Lord requires that "every decision made by either of these quorums must be by the unanimous voice of the same" and that "the decisions of these quorums . . . are to be made in all righteousness, in holiness, and lowliness of heart, meekness and long suffering, and in faith, and virtue, and knowledge, temperance, patience, godliness, brotherly kindness and charity" (D&C 107:27, 30). This we earnestly strive to do.

We know that we hold the power of the priesthood "in connection with all those who have received a dispensation at any time from the beginning of the creation" (D&C 112:31). We think of those who have preceded us in these sacred offices, and at times we feel their presence.

We are overcome with what the Lord said of those who hold these sacred callings: "Whatsoever they shall speak when moved upon by the Holy Ghost shall be scripture, shall be the will of the Lord, shall be the mind of the Lord, shall be the word of the Lord, shall be the voice of the Lord, and the power of God unto salvation" (D&C 68:4).

Heed the Counsel of the Lord's Servants

During a very difficult time, the Lord gave the sternest warning that I know of in all scripture. It had to do with the building of the Nauvoo Temple. The Saints knew from experience that to proceed to build a temple would bring terrible persecution, so they delayed. The Lord extended the time and said, "If you do not these things at the end of the appointment ye shall be rejected as a church, with your dead, saith the Lord your God" (D&C 124:32).

Often overlooked in that revelation is a marvelous promise: "If my people will hearken unto my voice, and unto the voice of my servants whom I have appointed to lead my people, behold, verily I say unto you, they shall not be moved out of their place" (D&C 124:45).

Remember this promise; hold on to it. It should be a great comfort to those struggling to keep a family together in a society increasingly indifferent to, and even hostile toward, those standards which are essential to a happy family.

The promise is a restatement of what the Lord told the multitude: "Blessed are ye if ye shall give heed unto the words of these twelve whom I have chosen from among you to minister unto you, and to be your servants" (3 Nephi 12:1).

I repeat the promise that those who hearken to the voice of these men whom the Lord has raised up "shall not be moved out of their place" (D&C 124:45). But the promise was followed with this caution: "But if they will not hearken to my voice, nor unto the voice of these men whom I have appointed, they shall not be blest" (D&C 124:46).

A Special Witness That Jesus Is the Christ

The most precious thing we have to give is our witness of the Lord, our testimony of Jesus Christ.

I certify to you that the fourteen men with whom I share the ordination are indeed Apostles. In declaring this, I say no more than the Lord has taught, no more than may be revealed to anyone who seeks with a sincere heart and real intent for an individual witness of the Spirit.

These men are true servants of the Lord; give heed to their counsel. So, too, with the Seventy, who as especial witnesses carry an apostolic responsibility, and the Bishopric, worthy men of God. So, too, with the brethren and sisters across the world who are called to lead, who have earned that knowledge precious above all else.

4

THE AARONIC
PRIESTHOOD

I always like to arrive early for general priesthood meetings in order to shake hands with the deacons, teachers, and priests. I have to sift through a lot of elders, seventies, and high priests to find them, but it's well worth it to meet the bearers of the Aaronic Priesthood. We who hold the higher priesthood salute you, our brethren of the Aaronic Priesthood.

I want to tell you about the unseen power of the Aaronic Priesthood. A boy of twelve is old enough to learn about it. As you mature you should become very familiar with this guiding, protecting power.

Some think that unless a power is visible it cannot be real. I think I can convince you otherwise. Do you remember when you foolishly put your finger in that light socket? While you did not see exactly what happened, surely you felt it!

No one has ever seen electricity, not even a scientist with the finest instruments. However, like you, they have felt it. And we can see the

From an address given at general conference, October 3, 1981; see *Ensign,* Nov. 1981, 30–33.

results of it. We can measure it, control it, and produce light, and heat, and power. No one questions that it is real simply because he or she cannot see it.

Although you cannot see the power of the priesthood, you can feel it, and you can see the results of it. The priesthood can be a guiding and protecting power in your life. Let me give you an example.

After President Wilford Woodruff joined the Church, he desired to serve a mission. "I was but a Teacher," he wrote, "and it is not a Teacher's office to go abroad and preach. I dared not tell any of the authorities of the Church that I wanted to preach, lest they might think I was seeking for an office" (*Leaves from My Journal* [1882], 8).

He prayed to the Lord, and without disclosing his desire to any others, he was ordained a priest and sent on a mission. They went to the Arkansas Territory.

He and his companion struggled through a hundred miles of alligator-infested swamps, wet, muddy, and tired. Brother Woodruff developed a sharp pain in his knee and could go no farther. His companion left him sitting on a log and went home. Brother Woodruff knelt down in the mud and prayed for help. He was healed and continued his mission alone.

Three days later he arrived in Memphis, Tennessee, weary, hungry, and very muddy. He went to the largest inn and asked for something to eat and for a place to sleep, although he had no money to pay for either.

When the innkeeper found he was a preacher, he laughed and decided to have some fun with him. He offered Brother Woodruff a meal if he would preach to his friends. A large audience of the rich and fashionable people of Memphis gathered and were quite amused by this mud-stained missionary.

None would sing or pray, so Brother Woodruff did both. He knelt before them and begged the Lord to give him His Spirit and to show him the hearts of the people. And the Spirit came! Brother Woodruff

36

preached with great power. He was able to reveal the secret deeds of those who came to ridicule him.

When he was finished, no one laughed at this humble holder of the Aaronic Priesthood. Thereafter he was treated with kindness (see ibid., 16–18).

Wilford Woodruff was under the guiding, protecting power of his Aaronic Priesthood. The same power can be with you as well.

Let me teach you some very basic things about the Aaronic Priesthood.

It "is called the Priesthood of Aaron, because it was conferred upon Aaron and his seed, throughout all their generations" (D&C 107:13).

The Aaronic Priesthood goes by other names as well. Let me list them and tell you what they mean.

The Lesser Priesthood

First, the Aaronic Priesthood is sometimes called the lesser priesthood.

"Why is it called the lesser priesthood is because it is an append-age to the greater, or the Melchizedek Priesthood, and has power in administering outward ordinances" (D&C 107:14).

This means that the higher priesthood, the Melchizedek Priesthood, always presides over the Aaronic, or the lesser, Priesthood. Aaron was the high priest, or the presiding priest, of the Aaronic Priesthood. But Moses presided over Aaron because Moses held the Melchizedek Priesthood.

The fact that it is called the lesser priesthood does not diminish at all the importance of the Aaronic Priesthood. The Lord said it is necessary to the Melchizedek Priesthood (see D&C 84:29). Any holder of the higher priesthood should feel greatly honored to perform the ordinances of the Aaronic Priesthood, for they have great spiritual importance.

I have, as a member of the Quorum of the Twelve Apostles, passed the sacrament. I assure you I have felt honored and humbled beyond expression to do what some might consider a routine task.

The Levitical Priesthood

The Aaronic Priesthood is also called the Levitical Priesthood. The word *Levitical* comes from the name Levi, one of the twelve sons of Israel. Moses and Aaron, who were brothers, were Levites.

When the Aaronic Priesthood was given to Israel, Aaron and his sons received the *presiding* and administrative responsibility. The male members of all other Levite families were put in charge of the ceremonies of the tabernacle, including the Mosaic law of sacrifice.

The law of sacrifice had been observed since the days of Adam. It was symbolic of the redemption that would come with the sacrifice and the Atonement of the Messiah. The Mosaic law of sacrifice was fulfilled with the crucifixion of Christ.

Anciently God's covenant people looked forward to the Atonement of Christ through the ceremony of the sacrifice. We look back to that same event through the ordinance of the sacrament.

Both sacrifice before, and the sacrament afterward, are centered in Christ, the shedding of His blood, and the Atonement He made for our sins. Both then and now the authority to perform these ordinances belongs to the Aaronic Priesthood.

This is indeed a sacred responsibility and includes you in a brotherhood with those ancient servants of the Lord. It is no wonder that we feel so humble when we participate in the ordinances assigned to the Aaronic Priesthood.

Can you see that it is correct to call it the Aaronic or the Levitical Priesthood? It is a matter of designating duties; it is all one priesthood.

The Preparatory Priesthood

Finally, the Aaronic Priesthood is referred to as the preparatory priesthood. This, too, is a proper title because the Aaronic Priesthood prepares young men to hold the higher priesthood, to serve missions, and to be married in the temple.

I have thought it very symbolic that John the Baptist, a priest in the Aaronic Priesthood, prepared the way for the coming of the Lord in ancient times. He came also to restore the Aaronic Priesthood to the Prophet Joseph Smith and Oliver Cowdery to prepare for the coming of the higher priesthood. The Lord Himself said that "there hath not risen a greater than John the Baptist" (Matthew 11:11).

You would do well to watch your fathers and your leaders, to study how the Melchizedek Priesthood works. You are preparing to join the elders, seventies, high priests, and patriarchs and to serve as missionaries, quorum leaders, bishoprics, stake leaders, and as fathers of families.

A few of you who now sit in the congregation as deacons, teachers, and priests will one day sit on the stand as Apostles and prophets and will preside over the Church. You must be prepared.

It is indeed correct to call the Aaronic Priesthood the preparatory priesthood.

Priesthood Principles

Let me teach you some important principles of the priesthood. When you receive the Aaronic Priesthood, you receive all of it. There are three kinds of authority relating to your priesthood. You should understand them.

First, there is the priesthood itself. The ordination you received carries with it the overall authority to perform the ordinances and to possess the power of the Aaronic Priesthood.

Next, there are offices within the priesthood. Each has different privileges. Three of them—deacon, teacher, and priest—may be conferred upon you when you are in your teenage years. The fourth office, that of bishop, may come to you when you are mature and worthy to become a high priest as well.

The deacon is to watch over the church as a standing minister (see

D&C 84:111; 20:57–59). The quorum consists of twelve deacons (see D&C 107:85).

The teacher is to "watch over the church always, and be with and strengthen them" (D&C 20:53). The teachers quorum numbers twenty-four (see D&C 107:86).

The priest is to "preach, teach, expound, exhort, and baptize, and administer the sacrament, and visit the house of each member" (D&C 20:46–47). The priests quorum numbers forty-eight. The bishop is the president of the priests quorum (see D&C 107:87–88).

You always hold one of these offices. When you receive the next higher office, you still retain the authority of the first. For instance, when you become a priest, you still have authority to do all that you did as a deacon and teacher. Even when you receive the higher priesthood, you keep all of the authority of, and, with proper authorization, can act in the offices of, the lesser priesthood.

Elder LeGrand Richards, who was Presiding Bishop for fourteen years, often said, "I'm just a grown-up deacon."

There is no rigid form of wording for your ordination. It includes the conferring of the priesthood, the giving of an office, and also a special blessing.

I once attended a meeting with President Joseph Fielding Smith in which someone asked him about a letter that was then being circulated by an apostate who claimed that the Church had lost the priesthood because certain words had not been used when it was conferred. President Smith said, "Before we talk about his claim, let me tell you a little about the man himself." He then described the character of the man and concluded, "And so you see, that man is a liar pure and simple—well, maybe not so pure."

The offices are a part of the priesthood, but the priesthood is greater than any of the offices within it.

The priesthood is yours forever unless you disqualify yourself through transgression.

When we are active and faithful, we begin to understand the power of the priesthood.

There is one other kind of authority that comes to you if you are set apart as a quorum president. You then are given the keys of authority for that presidency.

You receive the priesthood, and the office you hold within the priesthood (deacon, teacher, and priest), by ordination. You receive the keys of presidency by setting apart.

When you become a deacon, your father may, and generally should, ordain you; or another who holds the proper priesthood could do it.

If you are called as president of your quorum, your bishopric would set you apart. You can receive the keys of presidency only from those who have received them. Unless your father is in the bishopric, he would not have those keys.

These keys of presidency are temporary. The priesthood, and the offices within it, are permanent.

One more thing: You can receive the priesthood only from one who has the authority and "it is known to the church that he has authority" (D&C 42:11).

The priesthood cannot be conferred like a diploma. It cannot be handed to you as a certificate. It cannot be delivered to you as a message or sent to you in a letter. It comes only by proper ordination. An authorized holder of the priesthood has to be there. He must place his hands upon your head and ordain you.

That is one reason why the General Authorities travel so much—to convey the keys of priesthood authority. Every stake president everywhere in the world has received his authority under the hands of one of the presiding brethren of the Church. There has never been one exception.

Remember these things. The priesthood is very, very precious to the Lord. He is very careful about how it is conferred, and by whom. It is never done in secret.

I have told you how the *authority* is given to you. The *power* you receive will depend on what you do with this sacred, unseen gift.

Your authority comes through your ordination; your power comes through obedience and worthiness.

Let me tell you how one of our sons learned obedience. When he was about deacon age, we went to his grandfather's ranch in Wyoming. He wanted to start breaking a horse he had been given. It had been running wild in the hills.

It took nearly all day to get the herd to the corral and to tie his horse up with a heavy halter and a rope.

I told him that his horse must stay tied there until it settled down; he could talk to it, carefully touch it, but he must not, under any circumstance, untie it.

We finally went in for our supper. He quickly ate and rushed back out to see his horse. Presently I heard him cry out. I knew what had happened. He had untied his horse. He was going to train it to lead. As the horse pulled away from him, he instinctively did something I had told him never, never to do. He looped the rope around his wrist to get a better grip.

As I ran from the house, I saw the horse go by. Our boy could not release the rope; he was being pulled with great leaping steps. And then he went down! If the horse had turned to the right, he would have been dragged out the gate and into the hills and would certainly have lost his life. It turned to the left, and for a moment was hung up in a fence corner—just long enough for me to loop the rope around a post and to free my son.

Then came a father-to-son chat! "Son, if you are ever going to control that horse, you will have to use something besides your muscles. The horse is bigger than you are, it is stronger than you are, and it always will be. Someday you may ride your horse if you train it to be

42

obedient, a lesson that you must learn yourself first." He had learned a very valuable lesson.

Two summers later we went again to the ranch to look for his horse. It had been running all winter with the wild herd. We found them in a meadow down by the river. I watched from a hillside as he and his sister moved carefully to the edge of the meadow. The horses moved nervously away. Then he whistled. His horse hesitated, then left the herd and trotted up to them.

My son had learned that there is great power in things that are not seen, such unseen things as obedience. Just as obedience to principle gave him power to train his horse, obedience to the priesthood has taught him to control himself.

Throughout your life you will belong to a quorum of the priesthood; your brethren will be a strength and a support to you. More than that—you will have the privilege of being a support to them.

Much of what I have told you about the Aaronic Priesthood applies to the Melchizedek Priesthood as well. The names of the offices change, more authority is given, but the principles remain the same.

Power in the priesthood comes from doing your duty in ordinary things: attending meetings, accepting assignments, reading the scriptures, keeping the Word of Wisdom.

President Woodruff said: "I traveled thousands of miles and preached the Gospel as a Priest, and, as I have said to congregations before, the Lord sustained me and made manifest His power in the defense of my life as much while I held that office as He has done while I have held the office of an Apostle. The Lord sustains any man that holds a portion of the Priesthood, whether he is a Priest, an Elder, a Seventy, or an Apostle, if he magnifies his calling and does his duty" (*Millennial Star,* 28 Sept. 1905, 610).

John the Baptist restored the Aaronic Priesthood with these words: "Upon you my fellow servants, in the name of Messiah I confer the Priesthood of Aaron, which holds the keys of the ministering of angels, and of the gospel of repentance, and of baptism by immersion for the remission of sins" (D&C 13:1).

Our deacons, teachers, and priests have been given sacred authority. May the angels minister unto you. May the power of the priesthood be upon you, our beloved young brethren, and upon your sons throughout the generations ahead. I bear witness that the gospel is true, that the priesthood holds great power, a guiding, protecting power for those who hold the Aaronic Priesthood.

5

A KINGDOM OF PRIESTS

I have in my possession a tiny, brown glass bottle. I have kept it since it was issued to me in the jungles of the Philippine Islands during World War II. It originally held Atabrine tablets, a medicine to prevent malaria. However, some of us Latter-day Saint servicemen removed the tablets, washed the bottle carefully, and used it for consecrated oil.

This tiny container of oil was a great strength to me. It represented the authority of the priesthood. It was a reminder of my responsibility to stay worthy to bless others.

Consider this example: A boy working in the field with his father was seriously injured. Among those who stopped and offered to help was a local businessman. The father recognized him as an elder in the Church. He carried a small container of oil much like this tiny bottle.

"Elder, will you please anoint my son?" the father asked.

Then the businessman obliged and poured a few drops of oil on the crown of the boy's head, laid his hands gently on his head, and

From an address given at a fireside for the 175th anniversary of the restoration of the Aaronic Priesthood, May 16, 2004.

said, "By virtue of the holy Melchizedek Priesthood, I anoint you with this oil, which has been consecrated for the anointing of the sick in the household of faith, in the name of Jesus Christ, amen."

The father then added his dusty hands and began, "By virtue of the holy Melchizedek Priesthood, we place our hands upon your head and seal this anointing and pronounce a blessing." Then followed a pleading blessing of a loving father to his Heavenly Father to bless his injured son. It was pronounced, also, in the name of Jesus Christ.

Such a scene is not uncommon in the Church today. It must seem very strange to passersby—ordinary men administering priestly ordinances. Both of these men, elders in Israel, belong to that "kingdom of priests" spoken of by the Lord to Moses the prophet, centuries ago:

"Now therefore, if ye will obey my voice indeed, and keep my covenant, then ye shall be a peculiar treasure unto me above all people: for all the earth is mine:

"And ye shall be unto me *a kingdom of priests,* and an holy nation" (Exodus 19:5–6; emphasis added).

The kingdom of God, The Church of Jesus Christ of Latter-day Saints, was restored to the earth (see D&C 65:2–6). And we *are* "a kingdom of priests."

Guided by divine revelation, the Prophet Joseph Smith did not organize the Church as other Christian churches were organized. What he did was different! Unusual! Courageous! Had he followed the pattern traditional in the other churches, we would not now be "a kingdom of priests."

The first section of the Doctrine and Covenants speaks of ordinary men given responsibility to carry on the work of the Lord:

"[The Lord] gave commandments . . . that it might be fulfilled, which was written by the prophets—

"The weak things of the world shall come forth and break down the mighty and strong ones, that man should not counsel his fellow man, neither trust in the arm of flesh—

"But that *every man might speak in the name of God the Lord, even the Savior of the world*" (D&C 1:18–20; emphasis added).

The phrase "that every man might speak in the name of God the Lord, even the Savior of the world" was the departure from Christian tradition.

Step by step the pattern was revealed. First the Aaronic Priesthood was restored by John the Baptist. Enfolded within it was the Levitical Priesthood (see D&C 13; Joseph Smith–History 1:68–73).

Subsequently, the Apostles Peter, James, and John, who were ordained by the Lord and were witnesses to His Crucifixion and who testified of His Resurrection, restored the Melchizedek or the greater priesthood, "the priesthood which is after the holiest order of God" (D&C 84:18) or "the Holy Priesthood, after the Order of the Son of God" (D&C 107:3). They restored the keys of the kingdom of God (see D&C 27:12–13). And we have since become "a kingdom of priests."

The visit of these four brethren connected the line of covenant priesthood authority to the restored Church. Since then an unbroken chain of prophets and apostles has conferred authority from one generation to the next.

The offices of the priesthood and the pattern of administration are defined by revelation. All of this was done, the revelation explains, "that faith also might increase in the earth;

"That mine everlasting covenant might be established;

"That the fulness of my gospel might be proclaimed by the *weak and the simple* unto the ends of the world, and before kings and rulers.

"Behold, I am God and have spoken it; these commandments are of me, and were given unto my servants in their weakness, *after the manner of their language,* that they might come to understanding" (D&C 1:21–24; emphasis added).

That is as it is today, for "the Lord doth grant unto all nations, of their own nation and tongue, to teach his word, yea, in wisdom, all that he seeth fit that they should have; therefore we see that the Lord doth counsel in wisdom, according to that which is just and true" (Alma 29:8).

Can you possibly imagine what it would be like to manage the Church today if we had to look for and hire ministers or pastors and then train them professionally and then provide them with a salary, regardless of how devout they might be? Can you see how difficult that would be in this very unsettled world?

In approximately 170 countries and 180 languages there is no need for that because the gospel was restored and the authority given, and we truly are "a kingdom of priests." Can anyone doubt that the Church was restored and that it is guided today by revelation both to leaders and to all of the members?

Do you men and boys understand how important you are to the work of the Lord? We are, all of us, just ordinary men. But having been given power by the priesthood, we have the commission to carry this work to every nation, kindred, tongue, and people (see Alma 29:8; D&C 133:37).

This sacred authority is placed in our keeping. It is conferred upon us by ordination, and offices are received by setting apart. It continues from our Prophet-President to you and to me. And because of the design that has been revealed, it can bless the lives of every individual who when brought to a knowledge of it can conform his life to the requirements of worthiness.

Again from section one: "And also those to whom these commandments were given, might have power to lay the foundation of this church, and to bring it forth out of obscurity and out of darkness, the only true and living church upon the face of the whole earth, with which I, the Lord, am well pleased, speaking unto the church collectively and not individually" (D&C 1:30).

The Church of Jesus Christ of Latter-day Saints is not just an adjustment of or a correction of what had become of Christianity following the great Apostasy. It is a replacement, a restoration of organization and authority to what had been when Christ established it.

Another revelation, the Word of Wisdom, confirms that ordinary men and women, though they be weak, can have part in this great work. It is essential to members of the Church to keep them open to spiritual communication, and it is defined as "a principle with promise, adapted to the capacity of the *weak and the weakest of all saints,* who are or can be called saints" (D&C 89:3; emphasis added). Keeping the Word of Wisdom (and we *must* keep it) will protect us from the destructive addictions which shackle us and interrupt our communication with our Heavenly Father.

You see why obeying the Word of Wisdom is set as a condition for ordination to the priesthood or entrance to the temple. *Ordinary* men (the weak ones spoken of) whose lives are in *order* can be *ordained* and can perform *ordinances.*

The Lord promised that "if men come unto me I will show unto them their weakness. I give unto men weakness that they may be humble; and my grace is sufficient for all men that humble themselves before me; for if they humble themselves before me, and have faith in me, then will I make weak things become strong unto them" (Ether 12:27).

Giving the Aaronic Priesthood to worthy boys and the Melchizedek Priesthood to worthy men shows the confidence our Heavenly Father has in us. It is a witness that we truly are His sons.

The Church is being established all over the world. It will work everywhere and anywhere. But there is a divine order to it.

We move from country to country teaching the gospel. Always there are those who accept the message. They are baptized and receive the gift of the Holy Ghost. The men make themselves worthy to receive the priesthood and the women to be called to serve. The Lord always leads us to them. Then the Church is established. How glorious to know that they have the power and authority to lead and to build up the Church. Man did not invent it. It has existed from all eternity. This "everlasting priesthood" (see Exodus 40:15; Numbers 25:13; D&C 128:17) is described in the revelations by such phrases as "from before the foundation of the world" or "from before the world was" (see D&C 124:38, 41; see also Alma 13:3).

We know the Lord trusts us; otherwise He would not give into our hands this great work and make of us "a kingdom of priests." That trust is very precious.

And now to the point of it all: The offices and the quorums and the auxiliaries which support them are cradled in the stakes and wards and missions and branches and continue the kingdom of God on the earth (see Matthew 6:33; Mark 1:14–15; D&C 65:2–6; 84: 34; 88:78; 105:32; 138:44). All of the offices and all of the ordinances have as their purpose the protection and exaltation of the family.

It was never intended that priesthood authority be limited to one man in a congregation but that every man as the head of his household become worthy to bless his family. The purpose of it all: the home and the family.

Brethren, you must be faithful to your wife and a protection to your children. You know the moral standard. You must keep it. Never neglect your wife or your children. Never abandon them. They are precious beyond any measure.

Ordinances were revealed and commandments were given to build temples, "for therein are the keys of the holy priesthood ordained" (D&C 124:34) that families can be sealed for time and for all eternity.

The work continues beyond mortal life. The ordinance of vicarious baptism makes it possible for everyone who has been born or will yet be born, who missed baptism during his or her life on earth, to come under its redeeming influence (see 1 Corinthians 15:29; D&C 124:29; 127:5–9; 138:33).

No person ever born to this earth, no matter where or when or what race or persuasion, will be overlooked or passed by or neglected.

All are provided for, either in this life or in the next, that "all mankind may be saved, by obedience to the laws and ordinances of the Gospel" (Articles of Faith 1:3).

The crowning principle of the gospel is the Atonement of the Lord Jesus Christ. He is the Messiah, the Mediator, the Redeemer.

As the "weak things of the world," we do the best we can. Through repentance, we can repair our mistakes. The doctrines of the Church teach us how to do that.

The Atonement of Christ provides for those things that we cannot ourselves make whole. Jesus Christ is the Son of God, the Only Begotten of the Father, our Savior, our Redeemer, and the Head of the Church which bears His name.

The example of the father blessing his injured son represents a noble example of priesthood authority. The elder assisting him represents the strength of the Church watching over every member and every family.

God bless all of us Aaronic Priesthood and Melchizedek Priesthood holders across the world—this great "kingdom of priests"—and the families which surround us.

6

COUNSEL TO YOUNG MEN

Young men speak of the future because they have no past, and old men speak of the past because they have no future. I am an old man, but I will speak to the young men of the Aaronic Priesthood about your future.

The Aaronic Priesthood you hold was restored by an angelic messenger. "The ordination was done by the hands of an angel, who announced himself as John, the same that is called John the Baptist in the New Testament. The angel explained that he was acting under the direction of Peter, James, and John, the ancient Apostles, who held the keys of the higher priesthood, which was called the Priesthood of Melchizedek" (Introduction to D&C 13).

"The power and authority of the lesser, or Aaronic Priesthood, is to hold the keys of the ministering of angels, and to administer in outward ordinances, the letter of the gospel, the baptism of repentance for

From an address given at general conference, April 4, 2009; see *Ensign*, May 2009, 49–51.

the remission of sins, agreeable to the covenants and commandments"
(D&C 107:20).

You have been ordained to an office in the priesthood of God and
given divine authority that is not and cannot be held by the kings and
magistrates and great men of this earth unless they humble themselves
and enter through the gate that leads to life eternal.

There are many accounts in the scriptures of young men serving.
Samuel served in the tabernacle with Eli (see 1 Samuel 1:24–28). David
was a young man when he faced Goliath (see 1 Samuel 17). Mormon's
service began when he was ten (see Mormon 1:2). Joseph Smith was
fourteen when he received the First Vision (see Joseph Smith—History
1:7). And Christ was twelve when He was found in the temple teaching the wise men (see Luke 2:41–52).

Paul told young Timothy, "Let no man despise thy youth"
(1 Timothy 4:12).

When I began my teaching career, President J. Reuben Clark Jr.,
the First Counselor in the First Presidency, had spoken to teachers. His
words went into my heart and influenced me ever since.

President Clark described youth as "hungry for things of the Spirit
[and] eager to learn the gospel." He said: "They want it straight, un-
diluted. They want to know . . . about our beliefs; they want to gain
testimonies of their truth. They are not now doubters but inquirers,
seekers after truth."

President Clark continued: "You do not have to sneak up behind
this spiritually experienced youth and whisper religion in [their] ears;
you can come right out, face to face, and talk with [them]. . . . You can
bring these truths to [them] openly. . . . There is no need for gradual
approaches" (*The Charted Course of the Church in Education* [pamphlet,
2004], 3, 9).

Since then I have taught young people in the same way that I teach
adults.

There are some things you need to understand.

The priesthood is something you cannot see nor hear nor touch, but it is a real authority and a real power.

When I was five years old, I became very ill. It turned out that I had polio, a disease that was completely unknown to the small-town doctor. I lay for several weeks on a World War I army cot in our front room beside a coal stove. Afterward, I could not walk. I remember very clearly sliding around on the linoleum floor and pulling myself up on chairs, learning to walk again. I was more fortunate than some. A friend walked with crutches and steel leg braces all of his life.

As I moved into school, I found that my muscles were weak. I was very self-conscious. I knew that I could never be an athlete.

It did not help a lot when I read about the man who went to a doctor to find a cure for his inferiority complex. After a careful examination, the doctor told him, "You don't have a complex. You really *are* inferior!"

With that for encouragement, I set about through life and determined to compensate in other ways.

I found hope in my patriarchal blessing. The patriarch, whom I had never met before, confirmed to me that patriarchs do have prophetic insight. He said that I had a desire to come to earth life and was willing to meet the tests that would accompany life in a mortal body. He said that I had been given a body of such physical proportion and fitness to enable my spirit to function through it unhampered by physical impediment. That encouraged me.

I learned that you should always take care of your body. Take nothing into your body that will harm it, such as we are counseled in the Word of Wisdom: tea, coffee, liquor, tobacco, or anything else that is habit-forming, addictive, or harmful.

Read section 89 in the Doctrine and Covenants. You will find great promises:

"All saints who remember to keep and do these sayings, walking in obedience to the commandments, shall receive health in their navel and marrow to their bones;

"And shall find wisdom and great treasures of knowledge, even hidden treasures;

"And shall run and not be weary, and shall walk and not faint."

And then this promise: "And I, the Lord, give unto them a promise, that the destroying angel shall pass by them, as the children of Israel, and not slay them" (D&C 89:18–21).

You may see others who seem to have been given a more perfect body than yours. Do not fall into the trap of feeling poorly about your height or weight or your features or your skin color or race.

You are a son of God. You lived in a premortal existence as an individual spirit child of heavenly parents. At the time of your birth, you received a mortal body of flesh and blood and bone in which to experience earth life. You will be tested as you prepare yourself to return to our Heavenly Father.

I ask you the same question that Paul asked the Corinthians: "What? know ye not that your body is the temple of the Holy Ghost which is in you, which ye have of God, and ye are not your own?" (1 Corinthians 6:19).

Your gender was determined in the premortal existence. You were born a male. You must treasure and protect the masculine part of your nature. You must have respectful, protective regard for all women and girls.

Do not abuse yourself. Never allow others to touch your body in a way that would be unworthy, and do not touch anyone else in any unworthy way.

Avoid the deadly poisons of pornography and narcotics. If these are in your life, beware! If allowed to continue, they can destroy you. Talk to your parents; talk to your bishop. They will know how to help you.

Do not decorate your body with tattoos or by piercing it to add jewels. Stay away from that.

Do not run with friends that worry your parents.

Everywhere present is the influence of Lucifer and his legion of angels. They tempt you to do those things and say those things and think those things that would destroy. Resist every impulse that will trouble your spirit (see Moroni 7:17).

You are not to be fearful. The Prophet Joseph Smith taught that "all beings who have bodies have power over those who have not" (*Teachings of Presidents of the Church: Joseph Smith* [2007], 211). And Lehi taught that all "men are instructed sufficiently that they know good from evil" (2 Nephi 2:5). Remember, the prayerful power of your spirit will protect you.

I remember when I was "[baptized] by immersion for the remission of sins" (Articles of Faith 1:4). That was appealing. I assumed that all my past mistakes were now washed away, and if I never made any more mistakes in my life, I would be clean. This I resolved to do. Somehow it did not turn out that way. I found that I made mistakes, not intentionally, but I made them. I once foolishly thought maybe I was baptized too soon. I did not understand that the ordinance of the sacrament, administered by you of the Aaronic Priesthood, is in fact a renewing of the covenant of baptism and the reinstating of the blessings connected with it. I did not see, as the revelations tell us, that I could "retain a remission of [my] sins" (Mosiah 4:12).

If you have been guilty of sin or mischief, you must learn about the power of the Atonement, how it works. And with deeply sincere repentance, you can unleash that power. It can rinse out all the small things, and with deep soaking and scrubbing, it will wash away serious transgression. There is nothing from which you cannot be made clean.

With you always is the Holy Ghost, which was conferred upon you at the time of your baptism and confirmation.

I was a priest in the Aaronic Priesthood when World War II exploded upon the world. I was ordained an elder when we were all marched away to war.

I had dreams of following an older brother, Leon, who at that time was flying B-24 bombers in the Battle of Britain. I volunteered for air force pilot training.

I failed the written test by one point. Then the sergeant remembered that there were several two-point questions, and if I got half right on two of them, I could pass.

Part of the test was multiple choice. One question was "What is ethylene glycol used for?" If I had not worked in my dad's service station, I would not have known that it is used for automobile antifreeze. And so I passed, barely.

I prayed about the physical. It turned out to be fairly routine.

You young men should not complain about schooling. Do not immerse yourself so much in the technical that you fail to learn things that are practical. Everything you can learn that is practical—in the house, in the kitchen cooking, in the yard—will be of benefit to you. Never complain about schooling. Study well, and attend always.

"The glory of God is intelligence, or, in other words, light and truth" (D&C 93:36).

"Whatever principle of intelligence we attain unto in this life, it will rise with us in the resurrection" (D&C 130:18).

We are to learn about "things that are above, and things that are beneath, things that are in the earth, and upon the earth, and in heaven" (D&C 101:34).

You can learn about fixing things and painting things and sewing things and whatever else is practical. That is worth doing. If it is not of particular benefit to you, it will help you when you are serving other people.

I ended up in the Orient, flying the same kind of bombers that my brother flew in England. My mission, as it turned out, was in teaching the gospel in Japan as a serviceman.

Perhaps the hardest challenge of war is living with uncertainties, not knowing how it will end or if we can go ahead with our lives.

I was issued a small serviceman's Book of Mormon that would fit into my pocket. I carried it everywhere; I read it; and it became part of me. Things that had been a question became certain to me.

The certainties of the gospel, the truth, once you understand it, will see you through these difficult times.

It was four years before we could return to our lives. But I had learned and had a sure testimony that God is our Father, that we are His children, and that the restored gospel of Jesus Christ is true.

Your generation is filled with uncertainties. A life of fun and games and expensive toys has come to an abrupt end. We move from a generation of ease and entertainment to a generation of hard work and responsibility. We do not know how long that will last.

The reality of life is now part of your priesthood responsibilities. It will not hurt you to want something and not have it. There is a maturing and disciplining that will be good for you. It will ensure that you can have a happy life and raise a happy family. These trials come with responsibility in the priesthood.

Perhaps you live in a country where most of what you eat and some of what you wear will depend on what can be produced by the family. It may be that what you can contribute will make the difference so that the rent is paid or the family is fed and housed. Learn to work and to support.

The very foundation of human life, of all society, is the family, established by the first commandment to Adam and Eve, our first parents: "Multiply, and replenish the earth" (Genesis 1:28; Abraham 4:28).

Thereafter came the commandment, "Honour thy father and thy mother: that thy days may be long upon the land which the Lord thy God giveth thee" (Exodus 20:12).

Be a responsible member of your family. Take care of your possessions—your clothing, your property. Do not be wasteful. Learn to be content.

It may seem that the world is in commotion; and it is! It may seem that there are wars and rumors of wars; and there are! It may seem that the future will hold trials and difficulties for you; and it will! However, fear is the opposite of faith. Do not be afraid! I do not fear.

7

THE RELIEF SOCIETY

It is my purpose to give unqualified endorsement to the Relief Society—to encourage all women to join in and attend, and priesthood leaders, at every level of administration, to act so that Relief Society will flourish.

The Relief Society was organized and named by prophets and apostles who acted under divine inspiration. It has an illustrious history. Always, it has dispensed encouragement and sustenance to those in need.

The tender hand of the sister gives a gentle touch of healing and encouragement which the hand of a man, however well intentioned, can never quite duplicate.

Relief Society inspires women and teaches them how to adorn their lives with those things which women need—things that are "lovely, or of good report or praiseworthy" (Articles of Faith 1:13). The First Presidency has urged women to attend "because in the work of the

From an address given at general conference, April 5, 1998; see *Ensign,* May 1998, 72–74.

Relief Society are intellectual, cultural, and spiritual values found in no other organization and sufficient for all general needs of its members" (*A Centenary of Relief Society* [1942], 7).

Relief Society guides mothers in nurturing their daughters and in cultivating in husbands and sons and brothers courtesy and courage and, indeed, all virtues essential to worthy manhood. It is quite as much in the interest of the men and boys that Relief Society prosper as in the interest of women and girls.

Some years ago Sister Packer and I were in Czechoslovakia, then behind the Iron Curtain. It was not easy to obtain visas, and we used great care so as not to jeopardize the safety and well-being of our members, who for generations had struggled to keep their faith alive under conditions of unspeakable oppression.

The most memorable meeting was held in an upper room. The blinds were drawn. Even at night, those attending came at different times, one from one direction and one from another, so as to not call attention to themselves.

There were in attendance twelve sisters. We sang the hymns of Zion from songbooks—words without music—printed more than fifty years before. The lesson was reverently given from the pages of a handmade manual. The few pages of Church literature we could get to them were typed at night, twelve carbon copies at a time, so as to share a few precious pages as widely as possible among the members.

I told those sisters that they belonged to the largest and by all measure the greatest women's organization on earth. I quoted the Prophet Joseph Smith when he and the Brethren organized the Relief Society: "I now turn the key in [behalf of all women]."

This society is organized "according to your natures. . . . You are now placed in a situation in which you can act according to those sympathies [within you]. . . .

"If you live up to [these] privileges, the angels cannot be restrained from being your associates. . . .

61

"If this Society listen[s] to the counsel of the Almighty, through the heads of the Church, they shall have power to command queens in their midst" (*History of The Church of Jesus Christ of Latter-day Saints,* 7 vols. [1932–1951], 4:607, 605).

The Spirit was there. The lovely sister who had conducted with gentility and reverence wept openly.

I told them that upon our return I was assigned to speak at a Relief Society conference; could I deliver a message from them? Several of them made notes; each expression, every one, was in the spirit of giving—not of asking for anything. I shall never forget what one sister wrote: "A small circle of sisters send their own hearts and thoughts to all the sisters and begs the Lord to help us go forward."

Those words, *circle of sisters,* inspired me. I could see them standing in a circle that reached beyond that room and circled the world. I caught the same vision the apostles and prophets before us have had. The Relief Society is more than a circle now; it is more like a fabric of lace spread across the continents.

The Relief Society works under the direction of the Melchizedek Priesthood, for "all other authorities or offices in the church are appendages to this priesthood" (D&C 107:5). It was organized "after the pattern of the priesthood" (Sarah M. Kimball, "Auto-biography," *Woman's Exponent,* 1 Sept. 1883, 51).

You sisters may be surprised to learn that the needs of men are seldom, if ever, discussed in priesthood quorums. Certainly they are not preoccupied with them. They discuss the gospel and the *priesthood* and the family! If you follow that pattern, you will not be preoccupied with the so-called needs of women.

There are many community causes worthy of your support. There are others which are flawed, for they erode those values essential to a happy family. Do not allow yourselves to be organized under another banner which cannot, in truth, fulfill your needs. Do not drift from the course established by the general presidency of the Relief Society. Their stated purpose is to help bring women and families to Christ.

As mission president, I attended a mission Relief Society conference. Our mission Relief Society president, a relatively recent convert, announced something of a course correction. Some local societies had strayed, and she invited them to conform more closely to the direction set by the general presidency of the Relief Society.

One sister in the congregation stood and defiantly told her that they were not willing to follow her counsel, saying they were an exception. A bit flustered, she turned to me for help. I didn't know what to do. I was not interested in facing a fierce woman. So I motioned for her to proceed. Then came the revelation!

This lovely Relief Society president, small and somewhat handicapped physically, said with gentle firmness: "Dear sister, we'd like not to take care of the exception first. We will take care of the rule first, and then we will see to the exceptions." The course correction was accepted.

Her advice is good for Relief Society and for priesthood quorums and for families. When you state a rule and include the exception in the same sentence, the exception is accepted first.

The brethren know they *belong* to a quorum of the priesthood. Too many sisters, however, think that Relief Society is merely a class to attend. The same sense of *belonging* to the Relief Society rather than just attending a class must be fostered in the heart of every woman. Sisters, you must graduate from *thinking* that you only *attend* Relief Society to *feeling* that you *belong* to it!

However much priesthood power and authority the men may possess—however much wisdom and experience they may accumulate—the safety of the family, the integrity of the doctrine, the ordinances, the covenants, indeed the future of the Church, rests equally upon the women. The defenses of the home and family are greatly reinforced when the wife and mother and daughters belong to Relief Society.

No man receives the fulness of the priesthood without a woman at his side. For no man, the Prophet said, can obtain the fulness of the priesthood outside the temple of the Lord (see D&C 131:1–3). And she is there beside him in that sacred place. She shares in all that he receives. The man and the woman individually receive the ordinances encompassed in the endowment. But the man cannot ascend to the highest ordinances—the sealing ordinances—without her at his side. No man achieves the supernal exalting status of worthy fatherhood except as a gift from his wife.

In the home and in the Church sisters should be esteemed for their very nature. Be careful lest you unknowingly foster influences and activities which tend to erase the masculine and feminine differences nature has established. A man, a father, can do much of what is usually assumed to be a woman's work. In turn, a wife and a mother can do much—and in time of need, most things—usually considered the responsibility of the man, without jeopardizing their distinct roles. Even so, leaders, and especially parents, should recognize that there is a distinct masculine nature and a distinct feminine nature essential to the foundation of the home and the family. Whatever disturbs or weakens or tends to erase that difference erodes the family and reduces the probability of happiness for all concerned.

There is a difference in the way the priesthood functions in the home as compared to the way it functions in the Church. In the Church our service is by call. In the home our service is by choice. A calling in the Church generally is temporary, for there comes a release. Our place in the home and family, which is based on choice, is forever and beyond.

In the Church there is a distinct line of authority. We serve where called by those who preside over us.

In the home it is a partnership with husband and wife equally yoked together, sharing in decisions, always working together. While the husband, the father, has responsibility to provide worthy and inspired leadership, his wife is neither behind him nor ahead of him but at his side.

The leaders of Relief Society, Young Women, and Primary are all members of the ward and stake councils, and they have a unity which comes from their membership in Relief Society. To the degree that leaders ignore the contribution and influence of these sisters in councils and in the home, the work of the priesthood itself is limited and weakened.

Neither the brethren, acting as a quorum of the priesthood, nor these sisters who sit in councils must ever lose—not for a minute can they lose—a perspective of the place of the home.

To serve the needs of an increasing number of dysfunctional families, the Church provides influences and activities to compensate for what is missing in those homes.

Priesthood and auxiliary leaders, and especially parents, must use wisdom born of inspiration to make very certain that those activities, for both leaders and members, are not overly demanding of time and money. If they are, it leaves too little of both and makes it difficult for attentive parents to influence their own children. Be very careful to sustain and support rather than supplant the home.

At those times when parents feel smothered and just cannot do it all, they must make wise and inspired judgments as to how much out-of-home activity of all kinds is best for their own family. It is on this subject that the priesthood leaders, in council assembled, must pay careful attention to the expressions of the sisters, the mothers.

Strong Relief Societies carry a powerful immunizing and healing influence for the mothers and the daughters, for the single parent, for the single sisters, for the aging, for the infirm.

You sisters who are called to serve in the Primary or the Young Women may miss the Relief Society class, but you do not really miss Relief Society; you belong to it. Many brethren serve the Aaronic

Priesthood members and miss their own quorum meetings. Do not feel denied; never complain about this unselfish service.

We watched our children and now watch our grandchildren leave for work or school in places far from the family. They take a little child or two and virtually nothing materially with which to establish a home.

How consoling it is to know that no matter where they go, a Church family awaits them. From the day they arrive, he will belong to a quorum of the priesthood and she will belong to Relief Society. There she will find a grandmother—someone to call in the place of her own mother when her cooking isn't turning out right or to ask how to know if a restless child is really ill. She will find the steady, wise hand of surrogate grandmothers. They will give a word of comfort when the painful disease of homesickness hangs on too long. The young family will find security—the husband in the quorums—the sister in Relief Society. Both have as their consummate purpose to secure the family eternally.

These lines are sung in the Relief Society:

> *As sisters in Zion, we'll all work together;*
> *The blessings of God on our labors we'll seek.*
> *We'll build up his kingdom with earnest endeavor;*
> *We'll comfort the weary and strengthen the weak.*
>
> *The errand of angels is given to women;*
> *And this is a gift that, as sisters, we claim:*
> *To do whatsoever is gentle and human,*
> *To cheer and to bless in humanity's name.*
>
> *How vast is our purpose, how broad is our mission,*
> *If we but fulfill it in spirit and deed.*
> *Oh, naught but the Spirit's divinest tuition*
> *Can give us the wisdom to truly succeed.*
> (Emily H. Woodmansee, "As Sisters in Zion,"
> *Hymns,* no. 309)

I conclude where I began—it is my purpose to endorse the Relief Society, to bear witness that Jesus is the Christ and that it was through inspiration that it was organized, and I invoke a blessing upon the sisters who attend it.

8

THE TEMPLE,
THE PRIESTHOOD

Just before the dedication of the Salt Lake Temple, President Wilford Woodruff and his counselors issued an epistle to the Saints. Although more than a hundred years have passed, it might have been issued today. They said:

"During the past eighteen months . . . political campaigns have been conducted, elections have been held. . . . We feel now that . . . before entering into the Temple to present ourselves before the Lord . . . , we shall divest ourselves of every harsh and unkind feeling. . . .

"Thus shall our supplications, undisturbed by a thought of discord, unitedly mount into the ears of Jehovah and draw down the choice blessings of the God of Heaven!" (Wilford Woodruff, George Q. Cannon, Joseph F. Smith, First Presidency of The Church of Jesus Christ of Latter-day Saints, 18 March 1893, quoted in James H. Anderson, "The Salt Lake Temple," *Contributor,* Apr. 1893, 284–85).

When the Salt Lake Temple was dedicated, it had been fifty-seven

---

From an address given at general conference, April 3, 1993; see *Ensign,* May 1993, 18–21.

years since the Lord appeared in the Kirtland Temple, keys were bestowed, and Elijah appeared, fulfilling the prophecy of Malachi twenty-two hundred years earlier.

There were to have been temples at Independence, at Far West, and on Spring Hill at Adam-ondi-Ahman, but those temples were never built.

It had been fifty-two years since the Lord had commanded the Saints to build a temple in Nauvoo and warned that if they did not complete it within the allotted time, "your baptisms for your dead shall not be acceptable unto me; and if you do not these things at the end of the appointment ye shall be rejected as a church, with your dead, saith the Lord your God" (D&C 124:32).

The Saints built the temple, but they were driven away, and it was destroyed by the mobs (see Don F. Colvin, "A Historical Study of the Mormon Temple at Nauvoo, Illinois," master's thesis, Aug. 1962, Brigham Young University).

Colonel Thomas L. Kane wrote: "They succeeded in parrying the last sword-thrust" of the mobs until "as a closing work, they placed on the entablature of the front . . .

"The House of the Lord:

"Built by The Church of Jesus Christ of Latter-day Saints.

"Holiness to the Lord!

" . . . It was this day," he wrote, that "saw the departure of the last elders, and the largest band that moved in one company together. The people of Iowa have told me, that from morning to night they passed westward like an endless procession. They did not seem greatly out of heart, they said; but, at the top of every hill before they disappeared, were to be seen looking back . . . on their abandoned homes, and the far-seen Temple and its glittering spire" ("Discourse Delivered before the Historical Society of Pennsylvania," 26 Mar. 1850, pamphlet, Church History Library).

The Saints disappeared beyond the western horizon, beyond Far

West, where the cornerstones set seven years earlier were still in place—led by prophets and apostles who held the keys of the priesthood and who carried in their minds the ordinances of the temple and the authority to administer the new and everlasting covenant.

When the Saints trickled into the Salt Lake Valley, all they owned, or could hope to get, was carried in a wagon, or they must make it themselves.

They marked off the temple site before even the rudest log home was built.

There was an architect in that first company, William Weeks, who had designed the Nauvoo Temple. But the hopeless desolation was too much for him. When President Young went east in 1848, Brother Weeks left, saying, "They will never build the temple without me" (see Thomas Bullock Journals, 1844–1850, 8 July 1848, Church History Library).

Truman O. Angell, a carpenter, was appointed to replace him. He said: "If the President and my brethren feel to sustain a poor worm of the dust like me to be Architect of the Church, let me . . . serve them and not disgrace myself. . . . May the Lord help me so to do" (Truman O. Angell Journal, 28 May 1867, Church History Library).

The isolation, which gave some relief from the mobs, was itself an obstacle. Where would they get sledgehammers and wedges with which to split out building blocks of granite? They didn't carry many of those in handcarts, or in wagon boxes, either.

In 1853 the cornerstone was set, and ox teams began dragging granite stones from the mountains twenty miles away.

"'Good morning, Brother,' one man was heard to say to a teamster. 'We missed you at the meetings yesterday afternoon.' 'Yes,' said the driver of the oxen, 'I did not attend meeting. I did not have clothes fit to go to meeting.' 'Well,' said the speaker, 'Brother Brigham called for some more men and teams to haul granite blocks for the Temple.'

"The driver, his whip thrown over his oxen, said, ' . . . We shall go and get another granite stone from the quarry'" (David O. McKay, Salt Lake Temple dedication services, 21 May 1963, 7–8).

President Woodruff had watched men cut out granite stones seventy feet square and split them into building blocks (Journal of Wilford Woodruff, 4 July 1889, Church History Library). If there was no mishap (and that would be an exception), that teamster, "too poorly clad to worship," could return within a week (David O. McKay, Salt Lake Temple dedication services, 21 May 1963, 7–8).

The wicked spirit, which had inspired Governor Boggs of Missouri to issue the order to exterminate the Saints and broods forever and always over the work of the Lord, had followed them west.

President Young had said when they entered the Valley: "If the people of the United States will let us alone for ten years, we will ask no odds of them" (Journal of Discourses, 26 vols. [1854–1886], 5:226). Ten years to the day a messenger arrived with word that Johnston's army was marching west with orders to "settle the Mormon question."

President Young told the Saints: "[We] have been driven from place to place; . . . we have been scattered and peeled. . . .

"We have transgressed no law, . . . neither do we intend to; but as for any nation's coming to destroy this people, God Almighty being my helper, they cannot come here" (Ibid).

The settlements were evacuated, and the Saints moved south. Every stone was cleared away from Temple Square. The foundation, which after seven years' work was nearing ground level, was covered over and the block was plowed.

Later, when the foundation was uncovered, they found a few cracks. It was torn out and replaced.

Sixteen large, inverted granite arches were built into the new foundation. There is no record as to why they did that. That manner of construction was unknown in this country then. If someday perchance there be a massive force wanting to lift the temple from beneath, then we shall know why they are there.

Construction inched upward. A young married couple might have visited the construction site and returned with teenage grandchildren to the yet unfinished temple.

As the temple neared completion, James F. Woods was sent to England to gather genealogies (see Abraham H. Cannon Journal, 13 July 1891, Harold B. Lee Library, Brigham Young University, Provo, Utah; hereafter cited as BYU Library), and it was the beginning of a sacred family history work beyond anything that man had ever imagined.

John Fairbanks and others were sent to France to learn to paint and to sculpt "so that the Lord's name may be glorified through . . . the arts" (John Fairbanks Diary, BYU Library). Brother Fairbanks left seven children for his wife to look after. He could not bear to part with her in public, so two of the children walked with him to the station for a tearful parting (see ibid).

Women contributed no less than the men to the building of the temple. Perhaps only another woman can know the sacrifice a woman makes to see that something that must be done, that she cannot do herself, is done. And only a good man knows in his heart of hearts the depth of his dependency upon his wife—how she alone makes what must be done worth doing.

In the throng on the day of dedication was a seven-year-old boy from Tooele who would carry a clear memory of that event and a clear memory of President Wilford Woodruff for another ninety years. LeGrand Richards would one day serve in the Quorum of the Twelve Apostles as his father before him had done.

When he was twelve, LeGrand heard President Woodruff give his last public address. Even after ninety years, Elder Richards bore clear testimony to us of those sacred events.

There have been many visitations to the temple. President Lorenzo Snow saw the Savior there. Most of these sacred experiences remain unpublished.

However imposing the Salt Lake Temple may be, the invisible temple within is the same in all temples. The ordinances are the same, the covenants equally binding, the Holy Spirit of Promise equally present.

On the day ground was broken for the Salt Lake Temple, President Brigham Young said: "Very few of the Elders of Israel, now on earth, . . . know the meaning of the word endowment. To know, they must experience; and to experience, a temple must be built" (*Discourses of Brigham Young,* comp. John A. Widtsoe [1999], 415–16).

The Lord, commanding the Saints to build the temple in Nauvoo, said:

"For there is not a place found on earth that he may come to and restore . . . the *fulness of the priesthood*" (D&C 124:28; emphasis added).

"I will show unto my servant Joseph all things pertaining to this house, and the *priesthood* thereof" (D&C 124:42; emphasis added).

"For therein are the *keys of the holy priesthood* ordained" (D&C 124:34; emphasis added).

Some members of the Church are now teaching that priesthood is some kind of a free-floating authority which can be assumed by anyone who has had the endowment. They claim this automatically gives one authority to perform priesthood ordinances. They take verses of scripture out of context and misinterpret statements of early leaders—for instance, the Prophet Joseph Smith—to sustain their claims.

What is puzzling is this: with all their searching through Church history, and their supposed knowledge of the scriptures, they have missed the one *simple, obvious, absolute* that has governed the bestowal of priesthood from the beginning, said as simply as this:

"We believe that a man must be called of God, by prophecy, and by the laying on of hands by those who are in authority, to preach the Gospel and administer in the ordinances thereof" (Articles of Faith 1:5).

The priesthood is conferred through ordination, not simply through making a covenant or receiving a blessing. It has been so since the beginning. Regardless of what they may assume or imply or infer from anything which has been said or written, past or present, specific ordination to an office in the priesthood is the way, and the only way, it has been or is now conferred.

And the scriptures make it very clear that the only valid conferring of the priesthood comes from "one who has authority, and it is known to the church that he has authority and has been regularly ordained by the heads of the church" (D&C 42:11).

Remember, it was the resurrected John the Baptist, "under the direction of Peter, James and John, who held the keys of the Priesthood of Melchizedek" (Joseph Smith—History 1:72) who came, in person, to restore the Aaronic Priesthood (see D&C 13), and it was the resurrected Peter, James, and John who came, in person, to restore the Melchizedek Priesthood (John came as a translated being; see D&C 7)—facts in Church history except for which our claim to priesthood authority would be invalid.

The Prophet Joseph Smith explained that the angel who appeared to Cornelius sent him to Peter to be taught because "Peter could baptize, and angels could not, so long as there were legal officers in the flesh holding the keys of the kingdom, or the authority of the priesthood"; and that while the Lord called Paul as "minister and . . . witness" on the road to Damascus (Acts 26:16), he sent him to Ananias to receive instruction and authority (*Teachings of the Prophet Joseph Smith,* comp. Joseph Fielding Smith [1976], 265).

The priesthood is an everlasting covenant. The Lord said: "All who will have a blessing at my hands shall abide the law which was appointed for that blessing, and the conditions thereof, as were instituted from before the *foundation of the world*" (D&C 132:5, emphasis added; see also D&C 124:33).

Do not miss that one simple, obvious absolute: The priesthood ever and always is conferred by ordination by one who holds proper authority, and it is known to the Church that he has it. And even when the priesthood has been conferred, an individual has no authority beyond that which belongs to the specific office to which one has been ordained. Those limits apply as well to an office to which one is set apart. Unauthorized ordinations or settings apart convey nothing, neither power nor authority of the priesthood.

If people seek to do mischief with the priesthood and with the sacred things of the temple, the Lord has said he would "blind their minds, that they may not understand his marvelous workings" (D&C 121:12).

In that epistle issued at the dedication of the Salt Lake Temple, the First Presidency also said:

"Can men and women who are violating a law of God, or those who are derelict in yielding obedience to His commands, expect that the mere going into His holy house and taking part in its dedication will render them worthy to receive, and cause them to receive, His blessing?

"Do they think that repentance and turning away from sin may be so lightly dispensed with?

"Do they dare, even in thought, thus to accuse our Father of injustice and partiality, and attribute to Him carelessness in the fulfillment of His own words?

"Assuredly no one claiming to belong to His people would be guilty of such a thing" ("The Salt Lake Temple," 284–85).

The Lord promised the Saints at Nauvoo:

"If ye labor with all your might, I will consecrate [the temple site] that it shall be made holy.

"And if my people will hearken unto my voice, and unto the voice of my servants whom I have appointed to lead my people, behold, verily I say unto you, they shall not be moved out of their place.

"But if they will not hearken to my voice, *nor unto the voice of these men whom I have appointed,* they shall not be blest" (D&C 124:44–46; emphasis added).

Say the word *temple.* Say it quietly and reverently. Say it over and over again. *Temple. Temple. Temple.* Add the word *holy. Holy Temple.* Say it as though it were capitalized, no matter where it appears in the sentence.

Temple. One other word is equal in importance to a Latter-day Saint: *Home.* Put the words *holy temple* and *home* together, and you have described the house of the Lord! May God grant that we may be worthy to enter there and receive the fulness of the blessings of His priesthood.

9

PRIESTHOOD POWER
IN THE HOME

When the Doctrine and Covenants was assembled, the revelations were pulled together by the Prophet Joseph Smith, who was then still in his twenties. A revelation was given as an introduction. It is now section one of the Doctrine and Covenants, although it was given much later than most of the revelations there. There is one phrase in that revelation that changed the work of the Church, and, if they will, changed the work of the Christian churches forever. That was simply "that every man might speak in the name of God the Lord, even the Savior of the world" (D&C 1:20).

To imagine putting together a church where the authority of the priesthood was to be given to every worthy adult male would seem like a very reckless, dangerous thing, but that is the way it is. So as we look at you across the world, you members of the Church, we are never afraid of the progress of the Church, because we know that there will

From an address given in the Worldwide Leadership Training Broadcast, February 11, 2012.

come by conversion and baptism a little group of brethren upon whom the fulness of the priesthood can be conferred.

Any elder holds as much priesthood as does the President of the Church or as I do as an Apostle—different offices. But the priesthood is not delegated out and parceled a little here and a little there. It is given all at once. In the ordinance where ordinations take place, the priesthood is conferred, and then the office is conferred. So a young man as young as eighteen planning to go on a mission has this ordinance, and they first say, "We confer upon you the Melchizedek Priesthood" and then ordain you to the office of elder in that priesthood.

That priesthood has some other titles: "The priesthood . . . after the holiest order of God" (D&C 84:18) and "the Holy Priesthood, after the Order of the Son of God" (D&C 107:3). It is the consummate power on this earth. It is the power by which the earth was created—and all other things in the vast universe that are a part of our life.

We know that every father can, or should, be an officer in the priesthood, meaning that he holds the priesthood and presides over his family in righteousness.

We are sometimes charged with being unkind to the sisters in that they do not hold the priesthood and therefore do not hold the offices that the brethren do. But it is well understood that whether or not we are exalted depends upon the sister who is at our side—the wife, the mother of our children—and no holder of the priesthood would in any way depreciate or mitigate the value and power of his wife. When I hear those comments that the sisters are less than the brethren, I wish that they could see inside the heart of every worthy holder of the priesthood and understand how he feels about his wife, the mother of his children—a reverence, not quite worship but a kind of worship, a respect for the companion in life that causes it to be that he can be exalted ultimately.

The Church is very practical in its organization. We are not confined to having one prelate or priest or pastor or vicar given authority then to rule over the congregation, but as that simple expression in the Doctrine and Covenants says, "Every man might speak in the name of God the Lord, even the Savior of the world" (D&C 1:20). We are very careful to set standards of worthiness so that when a man is prepared for the priesthood he must give up a lot of things that other men enjoy in life, and every one of them is a protection for him and his family. The Word of Wisdom was given at a time when the dangers of tea and coffee, liquor and tobacco, and all those things were not known. And yet the early brethren, bowing to what the Prophet said, would obediently accept the fact that there are standards if you are going to be ordained into the priesthood. And that is a great thing for a father, a husband, to live the gospel and teach it by example.

There is the responsibility in the Church that is permanent. We call a man to be a stake president or a bishop or some other presiding officer, and we pay proper respect for that authority, and yet the tenure of it is temporary. One day a stake president will be released, or a bishop will be released, but an elder is not released, and a high priest is not released, and a Seventy is not released. They hold that authority, and the honor of presiding over a family and being a father is eternal.

That gives me a lot of comfort at my young age when we have been married for more than sixty-five years, and I think that could come to an end. Then I realize that the gospel is true, and it will never come to an end. I have been very careful, and am very careful, to treat my wife with that respect and reverence that is due her in performing that thing that is of most worth for a woman in this life—to live the gospel, to be the wife and the mother of the children of a worthy holder of the priesthood.

In putting the Church together, the priesthood was restored, the Aaronic Priesthood first and then the Melchizedek Priesthood. The Church was not given all at once as a blueprint that the Prophet could just look at and then announce. It came "line upon line, precept upon precept, here a little and there a little" (2 Nephi 28:30; see also D&C

128:21). But as it came together in the fulness of time, we finally had it all restored.

We perform ordinances "in the name of Jesus Christ." There are one or two that vary from that a little. One of them, interestingly enough, is baptism, where the prayer says, "I baptize you in the name of the Father, and of the Son, and of the Holy Ghost" (3 Nephi 11:25; D&C 20:73). There are some ordinances in the temple that are expressed the same way. So everything that can be given is given, and in due time, we come to know our Father in Heaven, a loving Father whose concern for us is such that He rejoices at our happiness and, I am sure, sheds tears for our disobedience and mistakes.

When we have children of our own and hold the priesthood and those two things are together in our life, then we know what the fulness of the gospel of Jesus Christ is about, and we know who He is: Christ, the Son of God, the Only Begotten of the Father, who wrought the Atonement through which we can have erased all of the mistakes we have made in life and stand clean and pure before the Father in that day of judgment.

It is an interesting thing that across the world "every man might speak in the name of God the Lord, even the Savior of the world" (D&C 1:20).

You out there speaking languages, one or two of you speak in many languages. I have known one or two of the General Authorities that just seem to inhale languages. With Jacob de Jager, I used to travel with him, and we went to China and to other places. It just seemed like he stepped off the plane and took a deep breath, and he could speak the language and speak it well.

We can that way have men better than we are in many ways leading the Church out there and adequate and complete because they are attached to the powers of heaven. They are looked after by the arm of the Almighty and know that Jesus Christ, the Only Begotten of the

Father, is the head of the Church. We are His servants, all of us, and we are His sons, and we are His daughters.

It is a source of great comfort to me to know that as I go through life and make mistakes. I have said I wish that my last mistake was my worst one and my next mistake would not come. I do not have hope of either. You make mistakes and look back on your life and wonder, "Well, where am I now near the end of my life to face the judgment?" That does not worry me because I have repented and taken hold of that great Atonement that is offered by living the gospel of Jesus Christ.

As a holder of the priesthood, we respond to every call that comes to perform every service that will come, the most important of which is within the walls of our home. The last few Presidents of the Church, conscious of what the adversary was doing, have centered their teaching, their preaching on the home and the family. The Church is made up of families. We talk about the organization and how many wards and stakes we have, and they are incidental and temporary. When we talk about how many families we have, then we see the real growth in the Church.

I have lived a long time. I have traveled widely—two and a half million miles in the countries across the world. Many of them I have visited dozens of times. I have learned that we are the children of God, and I have come to know that the gospel of Jesus Christ is true. God lives; Jesus is the Christ, the Son of God, the Only Begotten of the Father; and all that we do, we do in His name as His agents. And what we do as His agents in governing the Church as an Apostle or in guiding a ward as a bishop or in serving as a counselor in an elders quorum presidency—all of these are secondary to being a father and a husband who holds the priesthood and lives worthily of it. That is the source of happiness and the great achievement in mortality.

The Family

The ultimate end of all activity in the Church is that a man and his wife and their children can be happy at home.

10

THE PROCLAMATION
ON THE FAMILY

Transcendent Ideas

The Church of Jesus Christ of Latter-day Saints is the restored Church, and the initial introduction was the appearance of the Father and the Son to the Prophet Joseph Smith. In that great First Vision, as we refer to it now, two great transcendent ideas were revealed that have guided the Church ever since.

The first: He is the Father. Of all the titles that God might have given to Himself, He chose the one that's closest to all of us. He is our Father. We accept that—that we are the children of God. And with the Son being there, it became a family introduction. And so the Father and the Son appeared.

In a revelation given shortly thereafter, the Lord said, "Wherefore, I the Lord, knowing the calamity which should come upon the inhabitants of the earth, called upon my servant Joseph Smith, Jun., and

---

From an address given in the Worldwide Leadership Training Broadcast, February 9, 2008.

spake unto him from heaven, and gave him commandments" (D&C 1:17).

Living by Revelation

And that was a beginning. It was the pattern, that we are to act and organize and live according to the revelations that the Lord has given. These revelations, as you know, compiled in the book of the Doctrine and Covenants and the revelations in the Book of Mormon and Pearl of Great Price, form the scriptural foundation for the Church.

We found that the Lord did not organize the Church according to the patterns of the other churches of the world. That is, there is no professional clergy. We don't have seminaries as such to prepare clergymen or clergywomen to guide the Church.

We find in that an equality of the brethren who hold the priesthood and the women who stand at their side. We work together, and we're organized first as families. We all have the right to inspiration and revelation, and oh, how we need it in this world, especially in the great challenge of raising a family.

Raising a Righteous Posterity

The first commandment given to Adam and Eve was that they were to multiply and replenish the earth, and the processes of multiplying and replenishing the earth were given to them in their bodies. And that pattern would continue through all of the annals of human history.

So we had the first family—Adam and his wife, Eve, and then their children. We know that there had been a war in heaven and that there had been a rebellion and that Satan had been cast out. He was determined to destroy the works of the Almighty and was informed enough or wise enough or even inspired enough to know that the place where he should start his destruction was with the family. We see that in the account of Adam and Eve. Then, as the history of the Church unfolded, the responsibilities of parents and children emerged.

A Proclamation to the World

Not too many years ago there came a movement in the world having to do with the family. The United Nations called a council on the family in Beijing, China. We sent delegations to that council on the family and to other councils that were held. And then it was announced that one of them would be held near our headquarters, and we thought, "Well, if they are coming here, we had better proclaim ourselves."

A proclamation in the Church is a significant, major announcement. Very few of them have been issued from the beginning of the Church. They are significant; they are revelatory. At that time, the Brethren issued "The Family: A Proclamation to the World." It is scripturelike in its power.

When you wonder why we are the way we are and why we do the things we do and why we will not do some of the things that we will not do, you can find the authority for that in this proclamation on the family. There are times when we are accused of being intolerant because we won't accept and do the things that are supposed to be the norm in society. Well, the things we won't do, we won't do. And the things we won't do, we can't do, because the standard we follow is given of Him.

As we examine this proclamation more closely, see if you don't see in it the issues that are foremost in society, in politics, in government, in religion now that are causing the most concern and difficulty. You'll find answers there—and they are the answers of the Church.

"The Family: A Proclamation to the World"

"We, the First Presidency and the Council of the Twelve Apostles of The Church of Jesus Christ of Latter-day Saints, solemnly proclaim that marriage between a man and a woman is ordained of God and that the family is central to the Creator's plan for the eternal destiny of [all] His children." (Note: This and all other quotations from the proclamation come from "The Family: A Proclamation to the World," *Ensign,* Nov. 2010, 129.)

Premortal Existence

We know in the Church from the doctrines that have been revealed to us that we had a premortal existence. It didn't all begin with the population of the earth with humankind. And the doctrines of the gospel were not new when they were revealed to the Prophet Joseph Smith. They were from all eternity and will be for all eternity.

"All human beings—male and female—are created in the image of God. Each is a beloved spirit son or daughter of heavenly parents, and, as such, each has a divine nature and destiny. Gender is an essential characteristic of individual premortal, mortal, and eternal identity and purpose.

"In the premortal realm, spirit sons and daughters knew and worshipped God as their Eternal Father and accepted His plan by which His children could obtain a physical body and gain earthly experience to progress toward perfection and ultimately realize their divine destiny as heirs of eternal life. The divine plan of happiness enables family relationships to be perpetuated beyond the grave."

Note that the proclamation describes our Heavenly Father's plan of salvation as a "plan of happiness." It is described elsewhere, in the Book of Mormon, as the "great plan of happiness" (Alma 42:8).

"The divine plan of happiness enables family relationships to be perpetuated beyond the grave. Sacred ordinances and covenants available in holy temples make it possible for individuals to return to the presence of God and for families to be united eternally.

"The first commandment that God gave to Adam and Eve pertained to their potential for parenthood as husband and wife. We declare that God's commandment for His children to multiply and replenish the earth remains in force. We further declare that God has commanded that the sacred powers of procreation are to be employed only between man and woman, lawfully wedded as husband and wife."

You'll note that declarations such as this are challenged in our day. The world wants to change these things. We will not. We cannot. When you wonder who we are and why we are, remember that we have this pattern and we will follow it.

"We declare the means by which mortal life is created to be divinely appointed. We affirm the sanctity of life and of its importance in God's eternal plan."

Our positions on such things as divorce, abortion, and gender issues are stated and outlined in the revelations, and the proclamation on the family is the clearest statement that we find of those issues.

Parental Duties

"Husband and wife have a solemn responsibility to love and care for each other and for their children. 'Children are an heritage of the Lord' (Psalm 127:3). Parents have a sacred duty to rear their children in love and righteousness, to provide for their physical and spiritual needs, and to teach them to love and serve one another, observe the commandments of God, and be law-abiding citizens wherever they live. Husbands and wives—mothers and fathers—will be held accountable before God for the discharge of these obligations.

"The family is ordained of God. Marriage between man and woman is essential to His eternal plan."

And in the Church we recognize no other pattern for marriage—marriage is between man and woman.

"Children are entitled to birth within the bonds of matrimony, and to be reared by a father and a mother who honor marital vows with complete fidelity. Happiness in family life is most likely to be achieved when founded upon the teachings of the Lord Jesus Christ."

I've always felt that the ultimate end of all of the activities and programs of the Church rests in a man and a woman and their family being happy at home.

"Successful marriages and families are established and maintained on principles of faith, prayer, repentance, forgiveness, respect, love, compassion, work, and wholesome recreational activities. By divine design, fathers are to preside over their families in love and righteousness and are responsible to provide the necessities of life and protection for their families. Mothers are primarily responsible for the nurture of their children. In these sacred responsibilities, fathers and mothers are obligated to help one another as equal partners. Disability, death, or other circumstances may necessitate individual adaptation. Extended families should lend support when needed."

A Warning

"We warn"—we don't often use that word, but it's appropriate here—"We warn that individuals who violate covenants of chastity, who abuse spouse or offspring, or who fail to fulfill family responsibilities will one day stand accountable before God. Further, we warn that the disintegration of the family will bring upon individuals, communities, and nations the calamities foretold by ancient and modern prophets.

"We call upon responsible citizens and officers of government everywhere to promote those measures designed to maintain and strengthen the family as the fundamental unit of society."

Doctrines and Ordinances

Of course, there are many opportunities for practical applications and instruction and counsel and guidance, but they all come back to the revelations of the scriptures, to doctrine, and to the principles as proclaimed in this proclamation on the family.

When you young people who now look forward to marriage and a family life look around and see the dangers, you need to know that there is only one place on this earth where the family can be fully protected, and that's within the ordinances and the doctrines of the gospel of Jesus Christ. Live the gospel, and you're going to be all right.

The world isn't a very pleasant place to live in sometimes. There are challenges and disorders and patterns of life and death and all of the problems that come to us. It's not easy to establish a family in this life and to raise children. But with the Church as it is, you find the help that you need. The family is the fundamental unit of the Church, and all the activities of the Church are calculated to strengthen the family.

We know how to pray, we know how to teach, but there are times when we need help. Always, everywhere, there's a priesthood file leader. We've been taught the patterns of revelation and know that we have individual revelation. When we are unsure, we can turn to priesthood file leaders. If we follow them, we'll get safely through modern life with our children and our grandchildren.

Now, in our family we have grandchildren and great-grandchildren and still have the need to turn to the priesthood file leaders, to do what we are ordinarily expected to do in the Church. There are times of challenge and difficulty and danger and disappointment, but protecting families is what the Church is about. We do everything we can in the Church to protect families, relying upon the priesthood leadership, the power that's present everywhere in the world, in every nation where the Church exists—men who are ordained to the priesthood and women who are wise and maternal, with motherly instincts.

When our children left home to go a great distance and settle their family in a distant city, we saw them leave and had the comfort of knowing that they would have a family there. We told our children on more than one occasion, "You won't be able to telephone us very often because of the expense. But you will have a grandma there. Where will you find your grandma? In Relief Society. You'll have wise counsel and be able to have the same strength that you've had in our own family. So when you leave us for a new place, it just broadens the family circle."

Guidance and Blessings

When we're baptized into The Church of Jesus Christ of Latter-day Saints, there is another ordinance, separate from baptism, in which the gift of the Holy Ghost is conferred. Brethren holding the authority place their hands upon the head of each individual, each person who has been baptized, and confer upon him or her that gift, and it is to be a light and a teacher and a corrector and a guide as we move through life.

I don't think it's necessary for members of the Church to live in fear, to see all that's going on around us and say, "How can we ever raise a family when all of this temptation and difficulty is about us?"

You can, because you can be guided and you can teach your children to be guided. In all of that you can live a happy life and find in the consummation of all of this, in the next existence, that the family can be together.

I'm finding that old age is an interesting experience. I have wondered about the patterns of love and family association, the romantic love of youth. Will that be preserved? Oh, yes. That will not only be preserved but glorified and augmented.

Now, sometimes there are those that are lost. We have the promise of the prophets that they are not lost permanently, that if they are sealed in the temple ordinances and if the covenants are kept, in due time, after all the correction that's necessary to be given, they will not be lost.

I know that God lives, that He is our Father. He is our *Father!* I don't quite know how to say that word. It's a word we say almost glibly. But He's our Father; He loves us. And in that same pattern, we who lead the Church have that same feeling toward all who are members of the Church and all who might be. So I extend my blessings to all of you across the Church as you enjoy family life, either as parents or as children or in any pattern that is your pattern, that you'll be blessed and watched over, that the power of the Holy Ghost will be present in your life and the guarding power of the priesthood ever present will be there to correct you, to bless you, to boost you, and to confirm in you a testimony as you face the responsibility of raising up a righteous posterity.

11

PARENTS IN ZION

I have served in the Quorum of the Twelve Apostles for more than forty years. But I have another calling which I have held even longer. I am a parent—a father and a grandfather. It took years to earn the *grandfather* title—another twenty years the title of *great-grandfather*. These titles—*father, grandfather, mother, grandmother*—carry responsibility and an authority which comes in part from experience. Experience is a compelling teacher.

My calling in the priesthood defines my position in the Church; the title *grandfather,* my position in the family. I want to discuss both of them together.

Parenthood stands among the most important activities to which Latter-day Saints may devote themselves. Many members face conflicts as they struggle to balance their responsibility as parents together with faithful activity in the Church.

There are things vital to the well-being of a family which can be

---

From an address given at general conference, October 3, 1998; see *Ensign,* Nov. 1998, 22–24.

found only by going to Church. There is the priesthood, which empowers a man to lead and bless his wife and children, and covenants which bind them together forever.

The Church was commanded to "meet together often" (D&C 68:25) and told "when ye are assembled together ye shall instruct and edify each other" (D&C 43:8). Mosiah and Alma gave the same instruction to their people (see Mosiah 18:25; Alma 6:6).

We are commanded to "turn the heart[s] of the fathers to the children, and the heart[s] of the children to their fathers" (Malachi 4:6; see also 3 Nephi 25:5–6; D&C 2:2–3).

The Lord addressed Joseph Smith Jr. by name and said, "You have not kept the commandments, and must needs stand rebuked" (D&C 93:47). He had failed to teach his children. That is the only time the word *rebuke* is used in correcting him.

His counselor, Frederick G. Williams, was under the same condemnation: "You have not taught your children light and truth" (D&C 93:41–42). Sidney Rigdon was told the same thing, as was Bishop Newel K. Whitney (see D&C 93:44, 50), and the Lord added, "What I say unto one I say unto all" (D&C 93:49).

We have watched the standards of morality sink ever lower until now they are in a free fall. At the same time we have seen an outpouring of inspired guidance for parents and for families.

The whole of curriculum and all activities of the Church have been restructured and correlated with the home:

- Ward teaching became home teaching.
- Family home evening was reestablished.
- Genealogy was renamed family history and set to collect records of all the families.
- And then the historic proclamation on the family was issued by the First Presidency and the Council of the Twelve Apostles.

- The family became, and remains, a prevailing theme in meetings, conferences, and councils.
- All as a prelude to an era of building temples wherein the authority to seal families together forever is exercised.

Can you see the spirit of inspiration resting upon the servants of the Lord and upon parents? Can we withstand the challenge and the assault that is now leveled at the family?

In providing out-of-home activities for the family, we must use care; otherwise, we could be like a father determined to provide everything for his family. He devotes every energy to that end and succeeds; only then does he discover that what they needed most, to be together as a family, has been neglected. And he reaps sorrow in place of contentment.

How easy it is, in our desire to provide schedules of programs and activities, to overlook the responsibilities of the parent and the essential need for families to have time together.

We must be careful lest programs and activities of the Church become too heavy for some families to carry. The principles of the gospel, where understood and applied, strengthen and protect both individuals and families. Devotion to the family and devotion to the Church are not different and separate things.

I recently saw a woman respond when it was said of another, "Since she had the new baby, she isn't doing anything in the Church." You could almost see a baby in her arms as she protested with emotion: "She is doing something in the Church. She gave that baby life. She nurtures and teaches it. She is doing the most important thing that she can do in the Church."

How would you respond to this question: "Because of their handicapped child, she is confined to the home and he works two jobs to meet the extra expenses. They seldom attend—can we count them as active in the Church?"

And have you ever heard a woman say, "My husband is a very

good father, but he's never been a bishop or a stake president or done anything important in the Church." In response to that, a father vigorously said, "What is more important in the Church than being a good father?"

Faithful attendance at church, together with careful attention to the needs of the family, is a near-perfect combination. In Church we are taught the great plan of happiness (see Alma 12:32). At home we apply what we have learned. Every call, every service in the Church brings experience and valuable insights which carry over into family life.

Would our perspective be more clear if we could, for a moment, look upon parenthood as a calling in the Church? Actually, it is so much more than that; but if we could look at it that way for a moment, we could reach a better balance in the way we schedule families.

I do not want anyone to use what I say to excuse them in turning down an inspired call from the Lord. I *do* want to encourage leaders to carefully consider the home lest they issue calls or schedule activities which place an unnecessary burden on parents and families.

Recently I read a letter from a young couple whose callings in the Church frequently require them to hire a sitter for their small children in order for them to attend their meetings. It has become very difficult for both of them to be home with their children at the same time. Can you see something out of balance there?

Every time you schedule a youngster, you schedule a family—particularly the mother.

Consider the mother who, in addition to her own Church calling and that of her husband, must get her children ready and run from one activity to another. Some mothers become discouraged—even depressed. I receive letters using the word *guilt* because they cannot do it all.

Attending church is, or should be, a respite from the pressures of everyday life. It should bring peace and contentment. If it brings pressure and discouragement, then something is out of balance.

And the Church is not the only responsibility parents have. Other agencies have a very legitimate reason to call upon the resources of the family—schools, employers, community—all need to be balanced in.

Recently a mother told me her family had moved from a rural, scattered ward where, of necessity, activities were consolidated into one weekday night. It was wonderful. They had time for their family. I can see them sitting around the table together.

They moved west into a larger ward where members were closer to the chapel. She said, "Now our family is scheduled Tuesday night, Wednesday night, Thursday night, Friday night, Saturday night, and Sunday night. It is very hard on our family."

I repeat, when you schedule a youngster, you schedule a family— particularly the mother.

Most families try very hard; but some, when burdened with problems of health and finance, simply become exhausted trying to keep up, and eventually they withdraw into inactivity. They do not see that they are moving from the one best source of light and truth, of help with their family, into the shadows where danger and heartbreak await.

I must touch upon what must surely be the most difficult problem to solve. Some youngsters receive very little teaching and support at home. There is no question but that we must provide for them. But if we provide a constant schedule of activities sufficient to compensate for the loss in those homes, it may make it difficult for attentive parents to have time to be with and teach their own children. Only prayer and inspiration can lead us to find this difficult balance.

We often hear, "We must provide frequent and exciting activities lest our youth will go to less wholesome places." Some of them will. But I have the conviction that if we teach parents to be responsible and allow them sufficient time, over the long course their children will be at home.

There, at home, they can learn what cannot be effectively taught in either church or school. At home they can learn to work and to take responsibility. They learn what to do when they have children of their own.

For example, in the Church children are taught the principle of tithing, but it is at home that the principle is applied. At home even young children can be shown how to figure a tithe and how it is paid.

One time President and Sister Harold B. Lee were in our home. Sister Lee put a handful of pennies on a table before our young son. She had him slide the shiny ones to one side and said, "These are your tithing; these belong to the Lord. The others are yours to keep." He thoughtfully looked from one pile to the other and then said, "Don't you have any more dirty ones?" That was when the real teaching moment began!

The ward council is the perfect place to establish the balance between home and Church. Here the brethren of the priesthood, themselves fathers, and sisters of the auxiliaries, themselves mothers, can, with inspired insight, coordinate the work of the organizations, each of which serves different members of the family.

Members of the council can compare what each organization is providing for each member and how much time and money is required. They can unite rather than divide families and provide watch care over single parents, the childless, the unmarried, the elderly, the handicapped—and provide much more than just activities for the children and young people.

The ward council has resources often overlooked. For instance, grandparents, while not filling callings, can help young families who are finding their way along the same path they once walked.

The Lord warned parents, "Inasmuch as parents have children in Zion, . . . that teach them not to understand the doctrine of repentance, faith in Christ the Son of the living God, and of baptism and the gift of the Holy Ghost by the laying on of the hands, when eight years old, the sin be upon the heads of the parents" (D&C 68:25).

The ward council is ideal for our present need. Here the home and the family can be anchored in place, and the Church can support rather than supplant the parents. Fathers and mothers will understand both their obligation to teach their children and the blessings provided by the Church.

I have studied much in the scriptures and have taught from them. I have read much from what the prophets and apostles have spoken. They have had a profound influence upon me as a man and as a father.

But most of what I know about how our Father in Heaven really feels about us, His children, I have learned from the way I feel about my wife and my children and their children. This I have learned at home. I have learned it from my parents and from my wife's parents, from my beloved wife and from my children and therefore can testify of a loving Heavenly Father and of a redeeming Lord.

As the world grows ever more threatening, the powers of heaven draw ever closer to families and parents.

12

CHILDREN

Many years ago in Cuzco, high in the Andes Mountains of Peru, Elder A. Theodore Tuttle and I held a sacrament meeting in a long, narrow room with a door that opened onto the street. It was night and it was very cold.

While Elder Tuttle spoke, a little boy, perhaps six years old, appeared in the doorway. He was naked except for a ragged shirt that went about to his knees.

On our left was a small table with a plate of bread for the sacrament. This ragged street orphan saw the bread and inched slowly along the wall toward it. He was almost to the table when a woman on the aisle saw him. With a stern toss of her head, she banished him out into the night. I groaned within myself.

Later the boy returned. He crept along the wall, glancing from the bread to me. He was near the point where the woman would see him

From an address given at general conference, April 6, 2002; see *Ensign,* May 2002, 7–10.

again. I held out my arms, and he came running to me. I held him on my lap.

Then, as something symbolic, I set him in Elder Tuttle's chair. After the closing prayer, much to my sorrow, he darted out into the night.

When I returned home, I told President Spencer W. Kimball about him. He was deeply moved and spoke of it in a conference talk. He told others of it and said to me more than once, "That experience has far greater meaning than you have yet come to know."

I have never forgotten that little street orphan. Many times in South America I have looked for him in the faces of the people. When he comes back into my mind, others come with him.

After World War II on a cold night in a train station in southern Japan, I heard a tap on the train window. There stood a boy wearing the same ragged shirt, a rag tied about a swollen jaw, his head covered with scabies. He held a rusty tin can and a spoon, the symbol of an orphan beggar. As I struggled to open the door to give him money, the train pulled out. I will never forget that hungry little boy standing in the cold, holding up his empty tin can.

There was a sick little first grader in a hospital at a government Indian school with a fever and running nose. I opened a package from his mother, hundreds of miles away on the reservation. Wrapped in a cardboard box with an auto parts label, which no doubt she got from the trading post, were some Navajo fry bread and pieces of mutton—a Christmas present for her little boy.

On the news recently, I saw that long, familiar line of refugees. With them, as usual, were the children carrying children. One child was perched atop a massive bundle carried by her mother. As they pushed slowly and silently by, she looked into the camera. That sober little black face and those big black eyes seemed to ask, "Why?"

Children are the past, the present, and the future all blended into one. They are consummately precious. Every time a child is born, the world is renewed in innocence. I constantly think about and pray for the children and youth and their parents.

Recently, I attended a sacrament meeting given by children with special needs. Each was disabled in hearing or sight or mental development. Beside each was a teenager assigned as a companion. They sang and played music for us. Facing us on the front row was a young girl who stood and signed to those behind us who could not hear.

Jenny gave a brief testimony. Then her parents each spoke. They told of the utter agony they had known when they learned that their child would never have a normal life. They told of the endless, everyday trials that followed. When others would stare or laugh, Jenny's brothers put an arm protectively around her. The mother then told us of the love and absolute joy Jenny brought to the family.

Those parents have learned that "after much tribulation, . . . cometh the blessing" (D&C 103:12). I saw them bound together by adversity and refined into pure gold—true Latter-day Saints.

They told us Jenny adopts fathers. So when I shook hands with her, I said, "I'm a grandpa."

She looked up at me and said, "Well, I can see why!"

There is nothing in the scriptures, there is nothing in what we publish, there is nothing in what we believe or teach that gives license to parents or anyone else to neglect or abuse or molest our own or anyone else's children.

There is in the scriptures, there is in what we publish, there is in what we believe, there is in what we teach counsel, commandments, even warnings that we are to protect, to love, to care for, and to "teach [children] to walk in the ways of truth" (Mosiah 4:15). To betray them is utterly unthinkable.

Among the strongest warnings and the severest penalties in the revelations are those relating to little children. Jesus said, "But whoso shall offend one of these little ones which believe in me, it were better for him that a millstone were hanged about his neck, and that he were drowned in the depth of the sea" (Matthew 18:6).

In the days of the prophet Mormon, some who did not understand that little children are "blameless before God" (Mosiah 3:21) and are "alive in Christ" (Moroni 8:12) wanted to baptize little children. Mormon said they "[denied] the mercies of Christ, and [set] at naught the atonement of him and the power of his redemption" (Moroni 8:20).

Mormon sternly rebuked them, saying: "He that supposeth that little children need baptism is in the gall of bitterness and in the bonds of iniquity; for he hath neither faith, hope, nor charity; wherefore, should he be cut off while in the thought, he must go down to hell. . . .

"Behold, I speak with boldness, having authority from God" (Moroni 8:14, 16).

Only when children reach the age of accountability, set by the Lord at eight years of age (see D&C 68:27), is their baptism essential. Before that age, they are innocent.

Children should not be ignored or neglected. They absolutely must not be abused or molested. Children must not be abandoned or estranged by divorce. Parents are responsible to provide for their children.

The Lord said, "All children have claim upon their parents for their maintenance until they are of age" (D&C 83:4). We are to look after their physical, their spiritual, and their emotional needs. The Book of Mormon teaches, "Ye will not suffer your children that they go hungry, or naked; neither will ye suffer that they transgress the laws of God, and fight and quarrel one with another, and serve the devil, who is the master of sin, or who is the evil spirit which hath been spoken of by our fathers, he being an enemy to all righteousness" (Mosiah 4:14).

Nothing compares with a father who is responsible and in turn teaches his children responsibility. Nothing compares with a mother who is present with them to comfort them and give them assurance. Love, protection, and tenderness are all of consummate worth.

The Lord said, "I have commanded you to bring up your children in light and truth" (D&C 93:40).

All too often, a parent is left alone to raise children. The Lord has a way of strengthening that parent to meet alone what should be the responsibility of two parents. For either parent to deliberately abandon their children is a very grievous mistake.

I think often of another boy. We met him at a seminary graduation in a remote city in Argentina. He was well clothed and well nourished.

The students came down the aisle up to the stand. There were three rather high steps. He could not make the first step because his legs were too short. He was a dwarf.

It was then we noticed marching behind him two stalwart young men who stepped forward, one on either side, and lifted him gracefully to the podium. When the service was over, they lifted him down again and then marched out with him. They were his friends and watched over him. This boy could not reach the first step without being lifted up by his friends.

Those who come into the Church come as children spiritually. They need someone—some friend—to lift them up.

If we design the steps after baptism to fit only those who have long, strong legs, we ignore what the Lord said in the revelations. The prophets have told us that we "ought to be teachers, [and teach that] which be the first principles of the oracles of God; [for they are] such as have need of milk, and not of strong meat. . . .

" . . . Strong meat belongeth to them that are of full age, even those who by reason of use have their senses exercised to discern both good and evil" (Hebrews 5:12, 14).

The Apostle Paul wrote, "I have fed you with milk, and not with meat: for hitherto ye were not able to bear it, neither yet now are ye able" (1 Corinthians 3:2).

In a revelation given in 1830, just before the Church was organized, the Lord cautioned, "They cannot bear meat now, but milk they
must receive; wherefore, they must not know these things, lest they
perish" (D&C 19:22).

We must be careful lest we make that first step too high or design
it for those with strong, long legs and leave the others without some
friend to lift them up.

When some disciples rebuked those who brought little children,
"Jesus said, Suffer little children [*suffer* means to permit], and forbid
them not, to come unto me: for of such is the kingdom of heaven"
(Matthew 19:14).

When His disciples asked what kind of men they ought to be, Jesus
set a little child in their midst (see Matthew 18:2–3). Except we "become as a little child, [we] can in nowise inherit the kingdom of God"
(3 Nephi 11:38).

A deep concern for children and their parents is in my mind
and heart and soul. Over the years, I have wondered what President
Kimball meant when he reminded me of that street orphan in Cuzco
and repeated, "That experience has far greater meaning than you have
yet come to know." One day he added, "You held a nation on your
lap."

Now I understand what President Kimball was seeing; I know
what he meant. That boy in Cuzco and the one in Japan and the other
children about the world profoundly influence what I think and how I
feel and what I pray for most earnestly. I constantly think of little children and their parents who struggle to raise them in evermore perilous
times.

Like my Brethren, I have traveled all over the world. Like my
Brethren, I have held positions of trust in education, in business, in
government, and in the Church. I have written books and, like them,
have received honors, degrees, certificates, plaques. Such honors come
with the territory and are undeserved.

Assessing the value of those things, the one thing I treasure more than any of them—more than all of them put together—the thing of most value to me is how our sons and daughters and their husbands and wives treat their children and how, in turn, our grandchildren treat their little ones.

When it comes to understanding our relationship with our Heavenly Father, the things my wife and I have learned as parents and grandparents that are of most worth knowing, we have learned from our children.

This blessing has come to me as a gift from my wife. The Lord said of such women, "[A wife is given to a man] to multiply and replenish the earth, according to my commandment, and to fulfil the promise which was given by my Father before the foundation of the world, and for their exaltation in the eternal worlds, that they may bear the souls of men; for herein is the work of my Father continued, that he may be glorified" (D&C 132:63).

With women such as this to be the mothers of children, we see why the Lord revealed "that great things may be required at the hand of their fathers" (D&C 29:48).

I bear witness that the gospel is true, and the power of it is to bless little children. I pray earnestly that the children and youth and their parents will receive the gift of the Holy Ghost, that it will be a guide and a protection to them, that it will bear in their hearts the testimony that Jesus is the Christ, the Son of God, the Only Begotten of the Father.

13

CHILDREN OF GOD

The Twelve Apostles are called to "set in order" (D&C 107:58) and "regulate all the affairs of the [Church] in all nations" (D&C 107:33) under the direction of the First Presidency. That is not always easy to do.

I feel much as King Benjamin must have felt when he saw dangers among the people and said, "[I came not] to trifle with . . . words" (Mosiah 2:9). It can be very uncomfortable when we see thickening clouds and feel responsible to protect our families.

Nephi said, "I must speak concerning the doctrine of Christ; wherefore, I shall speak unto you plainly, . . . for my soul delighteth in plainness" (2 Nephi 31:2–3).

Whenever we speak of home and family and motherhood, we fear we might wound the tender hearts of those who may never marry or those whose marriages have failed. There are those who are greatly disappointed with their children. There are heartbreaking gender

From *Rise to the Divinity within You: Talks from the 2006 BYU Women's Conference* (Deseret Book, 2007), 1–11.

problems, untimely deaths, abortion, abuse, pornography, and, in addition, an endless list of things which almost dissuade us from speaking with the plainness that the scripture commands us to do.

I return, as I have on countless occasions, to the inspired words of a Relief Society president. I will ever be grateful to Sister Alberta Baker. A convert to the Church, she was mission Relief Society president when I was mission president in New England. She was a very small woman and walked with a very pronounced limp from childhood polio.

We had sixty Relief Societies scattered across the mission. Some of them were off course and some of them were little more than sewing circles and a few had lost their way entirely. Sister Belle Spafford, general president of the Relief Society, provided some simple guidelines that could be followed.

We called the Relief Society leaders together in the chapel at the Joseph Smith Birthplace Memorial in Vermont. I asked Sister Baker to explain the changes we were asking them to make. She gently invited the sisters to conform more closely to the patterns set for the Relief Society.

One sister stood and said defiantly, "That doesn't fit us. We're an exception!" She repeated with more emphasis, "We are an exception!"

It was a very tense moment, something of a crisis. Sister Baker turned to me for help. I was not interested in facing a fierce woman, so I motioned for her to proceed. Then came the revelation!

With gentle firmness, she said: "Dear sister, we'd like not to take care of the exception first. We will take care of the rule first, and then we will see to the exception." She continued to explain what a Relief Society should be.

Later I told her I would be quoting her all over the world. And so I have. In many challenging moments, some very tense, I have quoted the revelation that came to that sweet Relief Society president.

I will here address the rules first and later consider the exceptions.

I see in the tender hearts of women transcendent power. Listen to these words written by William Ross Wallace more than 125 years ago. They speak of you, and I agree with what they say:

Blessings on the hand of women!
Angels guard its strength and grace,
In the palace, cottage, hovel,
Oh, no matter where the place;
Would that never storms assailed it,
Rainbows ever gently curled;
For the hand that rocks the cradle
Is the hand that rules the world.

Infancy's the tender fountain,
Power may with beauty flow,
Mother's first to guide the streamlets,
From the souls unresting grow—
Grow on for the good or evil,
Sunshine streamed or evil hurled;
For the hand that rocks the cradle
Is the hand that rules the world.

Woman, how divine your mission
Here upon our natal sod!
Keep, oh, keep the young heart open
Always to the breath of God!
All true trophies of the ages
Are from mother-love impearled;
For the hand that rocks the cradle
Is the hand that rules the world.

Blessings on the hand of women!
Fathers, sons, and daughters cry,
And the sacred song is mingled
With the worship in the sky—

Mingles where no tempest darkens,
Rainbows evermore are hurled;
For the hand that rocks the cradle
Is the hand that rules the world.
("The Hand That Rocks the Cradle Is the Hand
That Rules the World," in *Poems that Live Forever,*
sel. Hazel Felleman [1965], 149–50.)

That is far more than just a poetic compliment. Later I will speak of an uncertain future in which mothers will be our protection.

President J. Reuben Clark Jr. described a pioneer family. Always last into camp at night, the wife was about to be a mother, the husband taking such care as he could to ease the jolting of the wagon. Then the baby came:

"Morning came when from out that last wagon floated the la-la of the newborn babe, and mother love made a shrine, and Father bowed in reverence before it. But the train must move on. So out into the dust and dirt the last wagon moved again, swaying and jolting, while Mother eased as best she could each pain-giving jolt so no harm might be done her, that she might be strong to feed the little one, bone of her bone, flesh of her flesh. Who will dare to say that angels did not cluster round and guard her and ease her rude bed, for she had given another choice spirit its mortal body that it might work out its God-given destiny?" ("They of the Last Wagon," *Improvement Era,* Nov. 1947, 705).

The rules and principles are in the scriptures. The revelations make it very clear that mankind is the offspring of heavenly parents. We have in God our Father and a heavenly mother the pattern of our parentage.

After being away four years, I came home from World War II and wanted, even yearned, to be married. In the years during the war, I became mature enough to realize that rather than making a list of specifications by which to measure a future companion, I should concentrate on what I myself must do. How could I be worthy of and able to fulfill the dreams of one with enduring values centered in home and family who would want to be my companion?

After more than fifty years, I am still trying to be worthy of her and good to her.

We were in school and had few material things to offer one another. We had our love and our faith and a determination to live the principles of the gospel—all of them, the difficult ones as well as the easy ones. We planned our life together and determined that we would accept each child born to us.

I remember clearly this incident: We had three small children. I had a very modest income. The bishop's wife, who was close to Donna's family (Donna's father was a counselor to the bishop), came to see her mother and said, "I've cried all morning. I heard that Donna is expecting again." We would not trade the child that came (it was our first girl), or the six that followed after, for anything you can imagine.

Once we said: "Perhaps if we plant a tree each time a child is born and pass that tradition to the coming generations, we may live in a small forest."

Now, several decades years later, it has come to pass in our children and grandchildren and great-grandchildren, who now number one short of 100. We live in a house that the real estate agents describe as old, sheltered under the trees at the end of a lane that reminds you of a forest.

I pay tribute to my wife. Now, I am bound to tell the truth. I have without hesitation described her as being perfect. And so she is! She has borne each of our ten children; each is a child of God. And now they and their partners to whom they are sealed, and the children, grandchildren, and great-grandchildren that have come, all honor her.

We got by during difficult years because my wife, in matters of food and clothing and shelter, was able to make something good and usable out of very little—sometimes out of almost nothing at all.

Some years ago, I returned home to find our little children were waiting in the driveway. They had discovered a newly hatched batch of chicks under the manger in the barn. When they reached for them, the mother hen, as mothers do, protected her brood. So they had come for reinforcements.

I soon gathered a handful of little chicks for them to see and to touch. There were black ones and yellow ones and brown ones and gray ones.

As our little girl held one of them, I said in a teasing way, "That little chick will make a nice watchdog when it grows up, won't it?" She looked at me quizzically, as if I didn't know much. So I changed my approach: "It won't be a watchdog, will it?"

She shook her head, "No, Daddy."

Then I added, "It will be a nice riding horse."

She wrinkled up her nose and gave me that "Oh, Dad!" look, for even a four-year-old knows that a chick will not be a dog or a horse or even a turkey; it will be a chicken. It will follow the pattern of its parentage. She knew that without having had a lesson or a lecture or a course in genetics.

No lesson is more manifest in nature than that all living things do as the Lord commanded them in the Creation. They reproduce after their own kind (see Moses 2:12, 24–25). They follow the pattern of their parentage. Everyone knows that. Every four-year-old knows that! A bird will not become an animal or a fish. A mammal will not beget a reptile, nor "do men gather . . . figs of thistles" (Matthew 7:16).

We are all children of God. It is just as simple as that! In all that you do as women, do not forget that we are all children of God. If you get that doctrine in place, with that rule established, it will serve you well in times when you are confronted with those who equate human-kind with animals.

I had another lesson from a child. Two of our little boys were wres-tling on the rug. They had reached that pitch—you know the one—where laughter turns to tears and play becomes strife. I worked a foot gently between them and lifted the older boy (then just four years of age) to a sitting position on the rug, saying, "Hey there, you monkey! You had better settle down."

He folded his little arms and looked at me with surprising seriousness. His little-boy feelings had been hurt, and he protested, "I not a monkey, Daddy. I a person!"

It is just that simple! I thought how deeply I loved him, how much I wanted him to be "a person," one of eternal worth, for "children are an heritage of the Lord" (Psalm 127:3). Each is a child of God. He is not a monkey; neither were his ancestors.

I have often thought that much of what I know that is most worth knowing I have learned from our children.

In the very beginning, God created both man and woman. He said, "It is not good that the man should be alone" (Genesis 2:18; Moses 3:18; Abraham 5:14) and "they twain shall be one flesh" (Matthew 19:5; Mark 10:8; D&C 49:16).

Our destiny is so established that man can find complete fulfillment and fill the divine purpose for his creation only with a woman to whom he is legally and lawfully married. The union of man and woman begets babies that are conceived and cross that frail footpath into mortality.

This divine pattern was planned and the gospel designed from "before the world was" (D&C 49:17). The plan provides for us to come to the world into a mortal body. It is "the great plan of happiness" (Alma 42:8). We did not design it. If we follow the pattern, happiness and joy will follow. The gospel and the moral standards are set to prevent us from straying into unworthy or unnatural behavior that will result in disappointment and unhappiness.

The virtue of tolerance has been distorted and elevated to a position of such prominence as to be thought equal to and even valued more than morality. It is one thing to be tolerant, even forgiving of individual conduct. It is quite another to collectively legislate and legalize to protect immoral conduct that can weaken, even destroy the family.

There is a dangerous trap when tolerance is exaggerated to protect the rights of those whose conduct endangers the family and injures the rights of the more part of the people. We are getting dangerously close to the condition described by the prophet Mosiah, who warned:

"Now it is not common that the voice of the people desireth anything contrary to that which is right; but it is common for the lesser part of the people to desire that which is not right; therefore this shall ye observe and make it your law—to do your business by the voice of the people.

"And if the time comes that the voice of the people doth choose iniquity, then is the time that the judgments of God will come upon you; yea, then is the time he will visit you with great destruction even as he has hitherto visited this land" (Mosiah 29:26–27).

Tolerance can be a dangerous trap.

The Prophet Joseph Smith said to the first Relief Society, "There must be decision of character, aside from sympathy" (*History of The Church of Jesus Christ of Latter-day Saints,* 7 vols. [1932–1951], 4:570).

It suits the purpose of the Almighty to let it be that some will not have a marriage or will find their marriages broken through death or mischief. Some have great difficulty having any children, and some will not have children of their own—that is, it will not happen in mortal life. But in the eternal scheme of things, it will happen as surely as the commandments are kept. Those yearnings unfulfilled in mortality will be filled to overflowing in the life beyond, where there is eternal love and eternal increase.

There is another dangerous trend as mothers, sometimes beyond their control, are being drawn out of the home. What could a mother possibly bring into the home that can equal her being at home with the children while they grow and mature?

We may learn from events of the future that "the hand that rocks the cradle is the hand that rules the world."

Some time ago there was printed in an international publication an article under the strange title of "Babies Win Wars" (Gunnar Heinsohn, *Wall Street Journal*, 6 March 2006). It chronicled several centuries of the history of countries that lost population. When they had difficulty in sustaining their population and themselves, they became vulnerable to invasion and occupation.

Now the birthrate is declining in every country in the world. In order for a nation's population to remain stable, the birthrate must be just over two children per woman of childbearing years.

In more than thirty countries in Europe, the birthrate is below the replacement rate. In several, it is hovering barely above half that replacement rate. The population of some countries is declining at an alarming rate.

The United States is barely above the replacement rate. Only because of immigration and the higher birthrate among the Hispanic people do we maintain our population.

All East Asian countries are currently below the replacement rate.

Latin America has witnessed a dramatic decline in birthrate in the past thirty years.

Virtually every social security and medical system in the developed world is facing bankruptcy. An aging population can neither work to sustain the people nor fight to protect them.

That trend is seen in the Church. Worldwide, the birthrate among members married in the temple is notably higher than in the world, but this rate too has been declining. In one European country with a sizeable population of Church members, for example, the birthrate among temple-married members, although higher than the national average, is below the replacement rate. Worldwide, the birthrate of Church members is only slightly higher than the world at large.

Like the rest of the population, members of the Church must suffer the consequences of these trends. We face a particular set of issues because the pool from which missionaries are drawn is in steady decline.

The First Presidency has written, "Marriage is ordained of God, and the paramount purpose of this sacred principle is to bring into the world immortal spirits to be reared in health and nobility of character, to fill the measure of their mortal existence" (First Presidency letterpress copybooks, 1 May 1939, Church History Library).

Mankind has gotten into an almost impossible predicament. In the ordinary home and the ordinary family, in almost every conceivable way, the destroyer leads humanity carefully away from the source of all happiness. The prophecy is now being fulfilled of wars and rumors of wars and plagues and pestilence (see Matthew 24:3–8).

Teach the children the plan of salvation, the sacredness of the body, the supernal nature of the power to give life. Mothers, guide them, warn them in your gentle way against misusing those sacred powers. The future of the family depends on how those powers are protected.

The devil has no body. He and his angels try to possess the bodies of mankind.

When the sacred power to give life is used immorally, unnaturally, or in perversion, one stands in jeopardy of failing the test of mortality. Even then, through true repentance, the mercy of the Holy One has power to reclaim and to heal.

"The hand that rocks the cradle [does rule] the world."

"The plan of redemption, which was prepared from the foundation of the world, through Christ" (Alma 22:13), was unfolded in the Creation. In the very beginning, man was created, and because "it is not good that the man should be alone," the Lord created a wife, "an help meet for him" (Genesis 2:18). In the scriptures, the word *meet* means *equal.* Man and woman are separate but equal, complementary to one another. Both the equal and the separate natures are essential to the onrolling of the great plan of happiness.

Do not envy a man his manhood or his priesthood. Foster and encourage, in every way you can, his role and the role of your sons in the destiny ordained for them.

To women is given a most supernal part of the plan of redemption. "And Adam called his wife's name Eve, because she was the mother of all living; for thus have I, the Lord God, called the first of all women" (Moses 4:26). Foster in yourself and in your daughters the exalted role of the woman, the incomparable gift of creation that attends motherhood.

The man was given to provide and protect; the woman was given to make it all worthwhile.

The ultimate end of all activity in the Church is that a man and his wife and their children can be happy at home, sealed together so that the family can continue throughout eternity.

This is the Church of Jesus Christ. He presides over it. His doctrines will lead us safely through all the difficulty and shadows that are ahead.

I bless you and your families—your companions in life, your children, grandchildren, and great-grandchildren—that you will understand the doctrines of the Church and be determined to live them, all of them. I promise you that you will be blessed, that you will be rewarded, and that you will be redeemed.

14

AND A LITTLE CHILD
SHALL LEAD THEM

I was stationed in Osaka, Japan, when World War II closed. The city was rubble, and the streets were littered with blocks, debris, and bomb craters. Although most of the trees had been blasted away, some few of them still stood with shattered limbs and trunks and had the courage to send forth a few twigs with leaves.

A tiny girl dressed in a ragged, colored kimono was busily gathering yellow sycamore leaves into a bouquet. The little child seemed unaware of the devastation that surrounded her as she scrambled over the rubble to add new leaves to her collection. She had found the one beauty left in her world. Perhaps I should say *she* was the beautiful part of her world. Somehow, to think of her increases my faith. Embodied in the child was hope.

Mormon taught that "little children are alive in Christ" (Moroni 8:12) and need not repent.

Around the turn of the previous century, two missionaries were

From an address given at general conference, March 31, 2012; see *Ensign,* May 2012, 6–9.

laboring in the mountains of the southern United States. One day, from a hilltop, they saw people gathering in a clearing far below. The missionaries did not often have many people to whom they might preach, so they made their way down to the clearing.

A little boy had drowned, and there was to be a funeral. His parents had sent for the minister to "say words" over their son. The missionaries stood back as the itinerant minister faced the grieving father and mother and began his sermon. If the parents expected to receive comfort from this man of the cloth, they would be disappointed.

He scolded them severely for not having had the little boy baptized. They had put it off because of one thing or another, and now it was too late. He told them very bluntly that their little boy had gone to hell. It was their fault. They were to blame for his endless torment.

After the sermon was over and the grave was covered, the elders approached the grieving parents. "We are servants of the Lord," they told the mother, "and we have come with a message for you." As the sobbing parents listened, the two elders read from the revelations and bore their testimony of the restoration of the keys for the redemption of both the living and the dead.

I have some sympathy for that preacher. He was doing the best he could with such light and knowledge as he had. But there is more that he should have been able to offer. There is the fulness of the gospel.

The elders came as comforters, as teachers, as servants of the Lord, as authorized ministers of the gospel of Jesus Christ.

These children of whom I spoke represent all of our Heavenly Father's children. "Children are an heritage of the Lord: and . . . happy is the man that hath his quiver full of them" (Psalm 127:3, 5).

The creation of life is a great responsibility for a married couple. It is the challenge of mortality to be a worthy and responsible parent. Neither man nor woman can bear children alone. It was meant that children have two parents—both a father and a mother. No other pattern or process can replace this one.

Long ago a woman tearfully told me that as a college student she had made a serious mistake with her boyfriend. He had arranged for an abortion. In due time they graduated and were married and had several other children. She told me how tormented she now was to look at her family, her beautiful children, and see in her mind the place, empty now, where that one child was missing.

If this couple understands and applies the Atonement, they will know that those experiences and the pain connected with them can be erased. No pain will last forever. It is not easy, but life was never meant to be either easy or fair. Repentance and the lasting hope that forgiveness brings will always be worth the effort.

Another young couple tearfully told me they had just come from a doctor where they were told they would be unable to have children of their own. They were brokenhearted with the news. They were surprised when I told them that they were actually quite fortunate. They wondered why I would say such a thing. I told them their state was infinitely better than that of other couples who were capable of being parents but who rejected and selfishly avoided that responsibility.

I told them, "At least you want children, and that desire will weigh heavily in your favor in your earthly lives and beyond because it will provide spiritual and emotional stability. Ultimately, you will be much better off because you wanted children and could not have them, as compared to those who could but would not have children."

Still others remain unmarried and therefore childless. Some, due to circumstances beyond their control, are raising children as single mothers or single fathers. These are temporary states. In the eternal scheme of things—not always in mortality—righteous yearning and longing will be fulfilled.

"If in this life only we have hope in Christ, we are of all men most miserable" (1 Corinthians 15:19).

The ultimate end of all activity in the Church is to see a husband and his wife and their children happy at home, protected by the principles and laws of the gospel, sealed safely in the covenants of the everlasting priesthood. Husbands and wives should understand that their first calling—from which they will never be released—is to one another and then to their children.

One of the great discoveries of parenthood is that we learn far more about what really matters from our children than we ever did from our parents. We come to recognize the truth in Isaiah's prophecy that "a little child shall lead them" (Isaiah 11:6).

In Jerusalem, "Jesus called a little child unto him, and set him in the midst of them,

"And said, Verily I say unto you, Except ye be converted, and become as little children, ye shall not enter into the kingdom of heaven.

"Whosoever therefore shall humble himself as this little child, the same is greatest in the kingdom of heaven" (Matthew 18:2–4).

"Jesus said, Suffer little children, and forbid them not, to come unto me: for of such is the kingdom of heaven.

"And he laid his hands on them, and departed thence" (Matthew 19:14–15).

We read in the Book of Mormon of the visit of Jesus Christ to the New World. He healed and blessed the people and commanded that the little children should be brought to Him.

Mormon records, "They brought their little children and set them down upon the ground round about him, and Jesus stood in the midst; and the multitude gave way till they had all been brought unto him" (3 Nephi 17:12).

He then commanded the people to kneel. With the children around Him, the Savior knelt and offered a prayer to our Father in Heaven. After the prayer the Savior wept, "and he took their little children, one by one, and blessed them, and prayed unto the Father for them.

"And when he had done this he wept again" (3 Nephi 17:21–22).

I can understand the feelings expressed by the Savior toward children. There is much to be learned from following His example in seeking to pray for, bless, and teach "those little ones" (3 Nephi 17:24).

I was number ten in a family of eleven children. So far as I know, neither my father nor my mother served in a prominent calling in the Church.

Our parents served faithfully in their most important calling—as parents. Our father led our home in righteousness, never with anger or fear. And the powerful example of our father was magnified by the tender counsel of our mother. The gospel is a powerful influence in the life of every one of us in the Packer family and to the next generation and the next generation and the next, as far as we have seen.

I hope to be judged as good a man as my father. Before I hear those words "well done" from my Heavenly Father, I hope to first hear them from my mortal father.

Many times I have puzzled over why I should be called as an Apostle and then as the President of the Quorum of the Twelve in spite of having come from a home where the father could be termed as less active. I am not the only member of the Twelve who fits that description.

Finally I could see and understand that it may have been because of that circumstance that I was called. And I could understand why in all that we do in the Church, we need to provide the way, as leaders, for parents and children to have time together as families. Priesthood leaders must be careful to make the Church family-friendly.

There are many things about living the gospel of Jesus Christ that cannot be measured by that which is counted or charted in records of attendance. We busy ourselves with buildings and budgets and programs and procedures. In so doing, it is possible to overlook the very spirit of the gospel of Jesus Christ.

Too often someone comes to me and says, "President Packer, wouldn't it be nice if . . . ?"

I usually stop them and say no, because I suspect that what follows will be a new activity or program that is going to add a burden of time and financial means on the family.

Family time is sacred time and should be protected and respected. We urge our members to show devotion to their families.

When we were first married, my wife and I decided that we would accept the children that would be born to us with the responsibility attending their birth and growth. In due time they have formed families of their own.

Twice in our marriage, at the time of the births of two of our little boys, we have had a doctor say, "I do not think you are going to keep this one."

Both times this brought the response from us that we would give our lives if our tiny son could keep his. In the course of that offer, it dawned on us that this same devotion is akin to what Heavenly Father feels about each of us. What a supernal thought.

Now in the sunset of our lives, Sister Packer and I understand and witness that our families can be forever. As we obey the commandments and live the gospel fully, we will be protected and blessed. With our children and grandchildren and great-grandchildren, our prayer is that each one of our growing family will have that same devotion toward those precious little ones.

Fathers and mothers, next time you cradle a newborn child in your arms, you can have an inner vision of the mysteries and purpose of life. You will better understand why the Church is as it is and why the family is the basic organization in time and in eternity. I bear witness that the gospel of Jesus Christ is true, that the plan of redemption, which has been called the plan of happiness, is a plan for families. I pray the Lord that the families of the Church will be blessed, parents and children, that this work will roll forth as the Father intends.

15

COUNSEL TO YOUTH

Youth are precious beyond measure. I have seen you in dozens of countries and on every continent. You are much better than we were when young. You know more about the gospel. You are more mature and more faithful.

You may wonder, at my age, what I can contribute to your lives. I have been where you are and know where you are going. With all that is going on in the world, with the lowering of moral standards, you young people are being raised in enemy territory.

We know from the scriptures that there was a war in heaven and that Lucifer rebelled and, with his followers, "was cast out into the earth" (Revelation 12:9). He is determined to disrupt our Heavenly Father's plan and seeks to control the minds and actions of all. This influence is spiritual, and he "is abroad in the land" (D&C 52:14).

From an address given at general conference, October 1, 2011; see *Ensign*, Nov. 2011, 16–19.

But despite the opposition, trials, and temptations, you need not fail or fear.

When I was seventeen, about ready to graduate from high school as a very average student with some handicaps, as I thought, everything around us came apart one Sunday morning. The next day we were called to the high school auditorium. On the stage was a chair with a small radio. The principal switched on the radio. We then heard the voice of President Franklin Delano Roosevelt as he announced that Pearl Harbor had been bombed. The United States was at war with Japan.

Later that scene was repeated. Again the voice of President Roosevelt, this time announcing that our country was at war with Germany. World War II had exploded across the world.

All at once our future was uncertain. We did not know what was ahead. Would we live to get married and have a family?

Today there are "wars and rumors of wars, and the whole earth [is] in commotion" (D&C 45:26). You, our youth, may feel uncertainty and insecurity in your lives. I want to counsel you and teach you and give you a warning about some things to do and some things not to do.

The gospel plan is "the great plan of happiness" (Alma 42:8). The family is the center of that plan. The family depends on the worthy use of those life-giving powers that are in your body.

Many of the temptations you face, certainly the most serious ones, relate to your body. You not only have power to create bodies for a new generation, but you also have agency.

The Prophet Joseph Smith taught, "All beings who have bodies have power over those who have not" (*Teachings of Presidents of the Church: Joseph Smith* [2007], 211). So every living soul who has a physical body ultimately has power over the adversary. You suffer temptations because of your physical nature, but you also have power over him and his angels.

By the time we graduated from high school, many of our classmates had marched away to war, some of them never to return. The rest of us were soon to enter the military. We did not know about our future. Would we survive the war? Would there be enough of the world left when we returned?

Against the certainty that I would be drafted, I joined the air force. Soon I was in Santa Ana, California, for preflight training.

I did not then have a firm testimony that the gospel was true, but I knew that my seminary teachers, Abel S. Rich and John P. Lillywhite, knew it was true. I had heard them testify, and I believed them. I thought to myself, "I will lean on their testimonies until I gain one of my own." And so it was.

I had heard about patriarchal blessings but had not received one. In each stake there is an ordained patriarch who has the spirit of prophecy and the spirit of revelation. He is authorized to give personal and private blessings to those who come recommended by their bishops. I wrote to my bishop for a recommend.

J. Roland Sandstrom was the ordained patriarch living in the Santa Ana stake. He knew nothing about me and had never seen me before, but he gave me my blessing. In it I found answers and instruction.

While patriarchal blessings are very private, I will share a short quote from mine: "You shall be guided through the whisperings of the Holy Spirit and you shall be warned of dangers. If you heed those warnings, our Heavenly Father will bless you so that you might again be united with your loved ones" (patriarchal blessing of Boyd K. Packer, given by J. Roland Sandstrom, 15 Jan. 1944).

That word *if*, though small in print, loomed as big as the page. I would be blessed to return from the war *if* I kept the commandments and *if* I heeded the promptings of the Holy Ghost. Although that gift had been conferred upon me at baptism, I did not yet know what the Holy Ghost was or how the promptings work.

What I needed to know about the promptings I found in the Book of Mormon. I read that "angels speak by the power of the Holy Ghost; wherefore, they speak the words of Christ. Wherefore, . . . feast upon the words of Christ; for behold, the words of Christ will tell you all things what ye should do" (2 Nephi 32:3).

Perhaps the single greatest thing I learned from reading the Book of Mormon is that the voice of the Spirit comes as a *feeling* rather than a sound. You will learn, as I have learned, to "listen" for that voice that is *felt* rather than *heard*.

Nephi scolded his older brothers, saying, "Ye have seen an angel, and he spake unto you; yea, ye have heard his voice from time to time; and he hath spoken unto you in a still small voice, but ye were past *feeling*, that ye could not *feel* his words" (1 Nephi 17:45; emphasis added).

Some critics have said that these verses are in error because you *hear* words; you do not *feel* them. But if you know anything at all about spiritual communication, you know that the best word to describe what takes place is the word *feeling*.

The gift of the Holy Ghost, if you consent, will guide and protect you and even correct your actions. It is a spiritual voice that comes into the mind as a thought or a feeling put into your heart.

The prophet Enos said, "The voice of the Lord came into my mind" (Enos 1:10).

And the Lord told Oliver Cowdery, "Behold, I will tell you in your mind and in your heart, by the Holy Ghost, which shall come upon you" (D&C 8:2).

It is not expected that you go through life without making mistakes, but you will not make a major mistake without first being warned by the promptings of the Spirit. This promise applies to all members of the Church.

Some will make critically serious mistakes, transgressing the laws of the gospel. Here it is time to remind you of the Atonement, repentance, and complete forgiveness to the point that you can become pure again. The Lord said, "Behold, he who has repented of his sins, the same is forgiven, and I, the Lord, remember them no more" (D&C 58:42).

If the adversary should take you prisoner due to misconduct, I remind you that you hold the key that will unlock the prison door from the inside. You can be washed clean through the atoning sacrifice of the Savior Jesus Christ.

You may in time of trouble think that you are not worth saving because you have made mistakes, big or little, and you think you are now lost. That is *never* true! Only repentance can heal what hurts. But repentance *can* heal what hurts, no matter what it is.

If you are slipping into things that you should not slip into or if you are associating with people who are pulling you away in the wrong direction, that is the time to assert your independence, your agency. Listen to the voice of the Spirit, and you will not be led astray.

I say again that youth today are being raised in enemy territory with a declining standard of morality. But as a servant of the Lord, I promise that you will be protected and shielded from the attacks of the adversary *if* you will heed the promptings that come from the Holy Spirit.

Dress modestly; talk reverently; listen to uplifting music. Avoid all immorality and personally degrading practices. Take hold of your life and order yourself to be valiant. Because we depend so much on you, you will be remarkably blessed. You are never far from the sight of your loving Heavenly Father.

The strength of my testimony has changed since I felt a need to lean on the testimonies of my seminary teachers. Today I lean on others when I walk due to age and childhood polio but not from doubts regarding spiritual matters. I have come to believe, to understand,

and to know the precious truths of the gospel and of the Savior Jesus Christ.

As one of His special witnesses, I testify that the outcome of this battle that began in the premortal life is not in question. Lucifer will lose.

You need not wander aimlessly to and fro, unsure of the path ahead. There are those who know the way. "Surely the Lord God will do nothing, but he revealeth his secret unto his servants the prophets" (Amos 3:7). The Lord organized His Church on the principle of keys and councils.

At the head of the Church sit fifteen men sustained as prophets, seers, and revelators. Each of the First Presidency and Quorum of the Twelve Apostles holds all of the priesthood keys necessary for directing the Church. The senior Apostle is prophet-President Thomas S. Monson, who is the only one authorized to exercise all of those keys.

The scriptures require that the First Presidency and Quorum of the Twelve work in councils and that the decisions of those councils be unanimous. And so it is. We trust the Lord to guide the way and seek only to do His will. We know that He has placed a great deal of trust in us, individually and collectively.

You must learn to "trust in the Lord with all thine heart; and lean not unto thine own understanding" (Proverbs 3:5). You must be trustworthy and surround yourself with friends who desire to be likewise.

Sometimes you might be tempted to think as I did from time to time in my youth: "The way things are going, the world's going to be over with. The end of the world is going to come before I get to where I should be." Not so! You can look forward to doing it right—getting married, having a family, seeing your children and grandchildren, maybe even great-grandchildren.

If you will follow these principles, you will be watched over and protected and you yourself will know by the promptings of the Holy Ghost which way to go, for "by the power of the Holy Ghost ye may know the truth of all things" (Moroni 10:5).

16

THE GOLDEN YEARS

Years ago on Christmas Eve, a cousin lost a little five-year-old boy to quick-pneumonia. The family gathered around the casket for the family prayer. A small blanket, made by his mother, lay folded across the little boy's feet.

Just as they were to close the casket, my mother stepped forward, put her arm around the grieving mother, and helped her unfold the blanket and tuck it around the little boy. The last his parents saw of their little son, he was asleep, covered with that favorite blanket. It was a very tender moment. That is what grandmothers do!

We returned to Brigham City for the funeral of my wife's father, William W. Smith. A young man I knew as a seminary student stood at the casket, deeply moved. I did not know that he knew my father-in-law.

He said: "One summer I worked for him on the farm. Brother Smith talked to me about going on a mission. My family could not

From an address given at general conference, April 6, 2003; see *Ensign*, May 2003, 82–84.

possibly support a missionary. Brother Smith told me to pray about it and said, 'If you decide to go on a mission, I will pay for your mission,' and he did."

Neither my wife nor her mother knew that. It was one of those things that grandfathers do.

We have ten children. One unsettled Sunday morning when our family was young, my wife was in sacrament meeting. As usual, I was away on Sunday. Our children took up much of a row.

Sister Walker, a lovely, gray-haired grandmother who had raised twelve children, quietly moved from several rows back and slid into the row among our restless children. After the meeting, my wife thanked her for the help.

Sister Walker said, "You have your hands full, don't you?" My wife nodded. Sister Walker then patted her on the hand and said, "Your hands full now; your heart full later!" How prophetic was her quiet comment. That is what grandmothers do!

We presided over the New England Mission. One of our missionaries married and had five children. He went away to get a larger car for his family and never returned. His body was later found under an overpass; his car had been stolen.

I called his stake president to offer help to the family. He had already offered.

The grandfather said, "We know what our duty is. We won't need any help from the Church. We know what our duty is." That is what grandfathers do!

The scriptures tell us, "With the ancient is wisdom; and in length of days understanding" (Job 12:12).

Once in a stake meeting, I noticed a larger than usual number of older members, most of them widows. I mentioned to the stake president how impressive they were.

The president replied, "Yes, but they are not active in the Church," meaning they did not serve as leaders or teachers. He spoke as though they were a burden.

I repeated his words, "Not active in the Church?" and asked, "Are they active in the gospel?" He did not quite understand the difference at first.

Like many of us, he concentrated so much on what people *do* that he overlooked what they *are,* a priceless resource of experience, wisdom, and inspiration.

We face an ominous challenge. Populations worldwide are declining. The birthrate in most countries is falling and life expectancy increasing. Families are smaller—deliberately limited. In some countries, in just a few years there will be more grandparents than there are children. The aging of the population has far-reaching consequences economically, socially, and spiritually. It will affect the growth of the Church.

We must teach our youth to draw close to the elderly grandpas and grandmas. The First Presidency has instructed young women approaching womanhood to join the mothers and grandmothers in Relief Society (see First Presidency letter, 19 Mar. 2003). Some young women draw away. They would rather be with those their own age.

Young women: Do not be so very foolish as to miss this association with the older sisters. They will bring more worth into your life than much of the activity you enjoy so much.

Leaders: Teach the girls to draw close to their mothers and grandmothers and to the older women in the Relief Society. They will then have an association similar to what the young men have in the priesthood quorums.

All of the attention given to our youth, all of the programs, all we do for them, will be incomplete unless we teach them the purpose of the Restoration. The keys of the priesthood were restored and the sealing authority revealed and temples built to tie the generations together. From ancient times through all the revelations runs that eternal, golden thread, "Turn the heart of the fathers to the children, and the heart of the children to their fathers" (Malachi 4:6).

Bishop: Do you realize that some problems you worry about so much with the youth, and with others, could be solved if they would stay close to their fathers and mothers and to their grandparents, to the older folks?

If you are burdened with overmuch counseling, there are older sisters, grandmas in the ward, who can influence young married women and act as a grandmother to them. And there are older grandfathers for the young men. Older people have a steadiness, a serenity that comes from experience. Learn to use that resource.

The Prophet Joseph Smith said, "The way to get along in any important matter is to gather unto yourselves wise men [and women], experienced and aged men [and women], to assist in council in all times of trouble" (*Teachings of the Prophet Joseph Smith,* comp. Joseph Fielding Smith [1976], 299).

We try to gather young people and miss getting the generations together. There is so much older members can do. If you see older members as inactive in the Church, ask yourself, "Are they active in the gospel?"

Do not overlook a great sustaining power in the prayers of the parents and the grandparents. Remember, the "fervent prayer of a righteous man [or woman] availeth much" (James 5:16).

Alma the Younger was a rebel. He was struck down by an angel who told him, "Behold, the Lord hath heard the prayers of his people, and also the prayers of his servant, Alma, who is thy father; for he has prayed with much faith concerning thee that thou mightest be brought to the knowledge of the truth; therefore, for this purpose have I come to convince thee of the power and authority of God, that the prayers of his servants might be answered according to their faith" (Mosiah 27:14).

My wife and I have seen our grandparents and then our parents leave us. Some experiences that we first thought to be burdens or trouble have long since been reclassified as blessings.

My wife's father died in our home. He needed constant care. Nurses taught our children how to care for our bedridden grandpa. What they learned is of great worth to them and to us. How grateful we are to have had him close to us.

We were repaid a thousand times over by the influence he had on our children. That was a great experience for our children, one I learned as a boy when Grandpa Packer died in our home.

Value the old folks for what they *are*, not just what they can *do*.

Have you ever wondered why the Lord organized the First Presidency and the Quorum of the Twelve Apostles so that the senior leadership of the Church will always be older men? This pattern of seniority values wisdom and experience over youth and physical vigor.

The average age of the Presidency and the Twelve at the present time is nearly eighty years old. We are not very nimble. We may be past our prime. Nevertheless, the Lord ordered it to be this way.

A conference or two ago, Joseph Wirthlin said he was going to challenge the members of the Twelve to a race. I thought once, "Well, I'll accept the challenge." Then I thought it would be safer to race against ninety-six-year-old Brother David Haight. I thought that over and decided that David might trip me with his cane, and I would lose the race. So I gave it up!

When the Presidency and the Twelve meet together, we combine 1,161 years of life with an astonishing variety of experiences. And we have 430 years cumulatively as General Authorities of the Church. Almost anything we talk about, one or more of us has been there, done that—including military action!

We live now in troubled times. In the lifetime of our youth, the troubles will never be less and will certainly be more. Old folks offer a sure knowledge that things can be endured.

Our children have married and left home to seek their fortunes.

One family drove away with an old car and their little children. My wife was in tears. I consoled her, saying, "The Church is where they are going. There will be a grandma there to answer her questions about cooking or nursing and a grandpa to teach him practical things."

An adopted grandma can be found in Relief Society. And a grandpa will be found in the quorums of the priesthood. But not all of the grandpas and grandmas are in the Church.

One son bought a small home in a distant state. He showed me bricks on a corner of the foundation that were eroding away. He asked what he should do.

I did not know, but I asked, "Is there an older couple that lives close to you?"

"Yes," he said, "across the street and down a few houses is a retired couple."

"Why don't you ask him to come over and look at that. He knows your climate."

That was done, and he got the advice of an older man who had seen problems like that and many others. That is what *adopted* grandpas can do.

"Honour thy father and thy mother: that thy days may be long upon the land which the Lord thy God giveth thee" (Exodus 20:12).

The Apostle Paul taught that "aged women" must teach young women and "aged men" must exhort young men, "shewing thyself a pattern of good works" (see Titus 2:1–7).

We are old now, and in due time, we will be summoned beyond the veil. We do not resist that. We try to teach the practical things we have learned over the years to those who are younger—to our family and to others.

We cannot *do* what we once did, but we have become more than ever we were before. Life's lessons, some of them very painful, qualify us to counsel, to correct, and even to warn our youth.

In your golden years there is so much to *do* and so much to *be*. Do not withdraw into a retirement from life, into amusement. That, for some, would be useless, even selfish. You may have served a mission and been released and consider yourself as having completed your service in the Church, but you are never released from being active in the gospel. "If," the Lord said, "ye have desires to serve God ye are called to the work" (D&C 4:3).

You may at last, when old and feeble, learn that the greatest mission of all is to strengthen your own family and the families of others, to seal the generations.

Now, I am teaching a true principle. I am teaching doctrine. It is written that "the principle [agrees] precisely with the doctrine which is commanded you in the revelation" (D&C 128:7).

In the hymn "How Firm a Foundation," which was published in 1835 in the first Latter-day Saint hymnbook, we find these words:

> E'en down to old age, all my people shall prove
> My sov'reign, eternal, unchangeable love;
> And then, when gray hair shall their temples adorn, . . .
> Like lambs shall they still in my bosom be borne.
> (*Hymns*, no. 85, v. 6)

Keep the fire of your testimony of the restored gospel and your witness of our Redeemer burning so brightly that our children can warm their hands by the fire of your faith. That is what grandfathers and grandmothers are to do!

17

DO NOT FEAR

One day our youngest son and his wife and family stopped by to see us. The first one out of the car was our two-year-old grandson. He came running to me with his arms outstretched, shouting, "Gwampa! Gwampa! Gwampa!"

He hugged my legs, and I looked down at that smiling face and those big, innocent eyes and thought, "What kind of a world awaits him?"

For a moment I had that feeling of anxiety, that fear of the future that so many parents express to us. Everywhere we go fathers and mothers worry about the future of their children in this very troubled world.

But then a feeling of assurance came over me. My fear of the future faded.

That guiding, comforting Spirit, with which we in the Church are so familiar, brought to my remembrance what I already knew. The fear of the future was gone. That bright-eyed, little two-year-old can have

From an address given at general conference, April 4, 2004; see *Ensign,* May 2004, 77–80.

a good life—a very good life—and so can his children and his grand-children, even though they will live in a world where there is much of wickedness.

They will see many events transpire in the course of their lifetime. Some of these shall tax their courage and extend their faith. But if they seek prayerfully for help and guidance, they shall be given power over adverse things. Such trials shall not be permitted to stand in the way of their progress, but instead shall act as stepping-stones to greater knowledge.

We do not fear the future for ourselves or for our children. We live in dangerously troubled times. The values that steadied mankind in earlier times are being tossed away.

We must not ignore Moroni's words when he saw our day and said, "Ye [must] awake to a sense of your awful situation" (Ether 8:24).

We cannot take lightly this warning from the Book of Mormon:

"The Lord in his great infinite goodness doth bless and prosper those who put their trust in him . . . doing all things for the welfare and happiness of his people; yea, then is the time that they do harden their hearts, and do forget the Lord their God, and do trample under their feet the Holy One—yea, and this because of their ease, and their exceedingly great prosperity.

"And thus we see that except the Lord doth chasten his people with many afflictions, yea, except he doth visit them with *death* and with *terror,* and with *famine* and with all manner of *pestilence,* they will not remember him" (Helaman 12:1–3; emphasis added).

Have you noticed that word *terror* in that prophetic Book of Mormon warning?

The moral values upon which civilization itself must depend spiral downward at an ever-increasing pace. Nevertheless, I do not fear the future.

World War I ended only six years before I was born. When we were children, the effects of the war were everywhere present. World

War II came only fifteen years later. And dark clouds were already gathering.

We had the same anxious feelings that many of you do now. We wondered what the future held for us in an unsettled world.

When I was a boy, childhood diseases appeared regularly in every community. When someone had chicken pox or measles or mumps, the health officer would visit the home and place a quarantine sign on the porch or in the window to warn everyone to stay away. In a large family like ours, those diseases would visit by relay, one child getting it from another, so the sign might stay up for weeks.

We could not blockade ourselves inside our homes or stay hidden away to avoid those terrible contagions. We had to go to school, to employment, or to church—to life!

Two of my sisters were stricken with very severe cases of measles. At first they seemed to recover. A few weeks later Mother glanced out of the window and saw Adele, the younger of the two, leaning against a swing. She was faint and weak with a fever. It was rheumatic fever! It came as a complication from measles. The other sister also had the fever.

There was little that could be done. In spite of all of the prayers of my parents, Adele died. She was eight years old.

While Nona, two years older, recovered, she had fragile health for most of her life.

When I was in the seventh grade, in a health class, the teacher read an article. A mother learned that the neighbor children had chicken pox. She faced the probability that her children would have it as well, perhaps one at a time. She determined to get it all over with at once.

So she sent her children to the neighbor's to play with their children to let them be exposed, and then she would be done with it. Imagine her horror when the doctor finally came and announced that it was not chicken pox the children had; it was smallpox.

The best thing to do then and what we must do now is to avoid places where there is danger of physical or spiritual contagion.

We have little concern that our grandchildren will get the measles. They have been immunized and can move freely without fear of that. While in much of the world measles has virtually been eradicated, it is still the leading cause of vaccine-preventable death in children. From money generously donated by Latter-day Saints, the Church recently donated a million dollars to a cooperative effort to immunize the children of Africa against measles. For one dollar, one child can be protected.

Parents now are concerned about the moral and spiritual diseases. These can have terrible complications when standards and values are abandoned. We must all take protective measures.

With the proper serum, the physical body is protected against disease. We can also protect our children from moral and spiritual diseases.

The word *inoculate* has two parts: *in*—"to be within"—and *oculate* means "eye to see."

When children are baptized and confirmed (see D&C 20:41, 43; 33:15), we place an *eye within them*—"the unspeakable gift of the Holy Ghost" (D&C 121:26). With the Restoration of the gospel came authority to confer this gift.

The Book of Mormon gives us the key:

"Angels speak by the power of the Holy Ghost; wherefore, they speak the words of Christ. . . . Feast upon the words of Christ; for behold, the words of Christ will tell you [and your children as well] all things what ye should do" (2 Nephi 32:3).

If you will accept it in your mind and cradle it in your feelings, a knowledge of the restored gospel and a testimony of Jesus Christ can spiritually immunize your children.

One thing is very clear: the safest place and the best protection against the moral and spiritual diseases is a stable home and family.

This has always been true; it will be true forever. We must keep that foremost in our minds.

The scriptures speak of "the shield of faith wherewith," the Lord said, "ye shall be able to quench all the fiery darts of the wicked" (D&C 27:17). This shield of faith is best fabricated in a cottage industry. While the shield can be polished in classes in the Church and in activities, it is meant to be handcrafted in the home and fitted to each individual.

The Lord said, "Take upon you my whole armor, that ye may be able to withstand the evil day, having done all, that ye may be able to stand" (D&C 27:15).

Our young people in many ways are much stronger and better than we were. They and we should not be afraid of what is ahead.

Encourage our young people. They need not live in fear (see D&C 6:36). Fear is the opposite of faith. While we cannot erase wickedness, we can produce young Latter-day Saints who, spiritually nourished, are immunized against evil influences.

As a grandfather who has lived a long time, I counsel you to have faith. Things have a way of working out. Stay close to the Church. Keep your children close to the Church.

In Alma's day "the preaching of the word had a great tendency to lead the people to do that which was just—yea, it . . . had more powerful effect upon the minds of the people than the sword, or anything else, which had happened unto them—therefore Alma thought it was expedient that they should try the virtue of the word of God" (Alma 31:5).

True doctrine, understood, changes attitudes and behavior. The study of the doctrines of the gospel will improve behavior quicker than a study of behavior will improve behavior.

Find happiness in ordinary things, and keep your sense of humor.

My sister Nona recovered from measles and rheumatic fever. She lived long enough to benefit from open heart surgery and enjoyed years of much improved health. Others spoke of her newly acquired energy. She said, "I have a Cadillac engine in a Model T frame."

Keep your sense of humor!

Do not be afraid to bring children into the world. We are under covenant to provide physical bodies so that spirits may enter mortality (see Genesis 1:28; Moses 2:28). Children are the future of the restored Church.

Put your homes in order. If Mother is working outside of the home, see if there are ways to change that, even a little. It may be very difficult to change at the present time. But analyze carefully and be prayerful (see D&C 9:8–9). Then expect to have inspiration, which is revelation (see D&C 8:2–3). Expect intervention from power from beyond the veil to help you move, in due time, to what is best for your family.

Each of us came into mortality to receive a mortal body and to be tested (see Abraham 3:24–26). Life will not be free from challenges, some of them bitter and hard to bear. We may wish to be spared all the trials of life, but that would be contrary to the great plan of happiness, "for it must needs be, that there is an opposition in all things" (2 Nephi 2:11). This testing is the source of our strength.

As an innocent child, my sister Adele's life was cruelly interrupted by disease and suffering. She and all the others so taken continue the work of the Lord beyond the veil. She will not be denied anything essential for her eternal progression.

We also lost an infant granddaughter. She was named Emma after my mother. We receive comfort from the scriptures: "Little children need no repentance, neither baptism. . . . Little children are alive in Christ" (Moroni 8:11–12).

Remember the Atonement of Christ. Do not despair or count as forever lost those who have fallen to the temptations of Satan. They will, after the debt is paid to "the uttermost farthing" (Matthew 5:26) and after the healing which attends complete repentance takes place, receive a salvation.

Follow the leaders who are called to preside over you, for the promise is given: "If my people will hearken unto my voice, and unto the voice of my servants whom I have appointed to lead my people, behold, verily I say unto you, they shall not be moved out of their place" (D&C 124:45).

The Church of Jesus Christ of Latter-day Saints will go forward "until it has filled the whole earth" (D&C 65:2) and the great Jehovah announces that His work is done (see Joseph Smith, *History of The Church of Jesus Christ of Latter-day Saints,* 7 vols. [1932–1951], 4:540). The Church is a safe harbor. We will be protected by justice and comforted by mercy (see Alma 34:15–16). No unhallowed hand can stay the progress of this work (see D&C 76:3).

We are not blind to the conditions in the world. The Apostle Paul prophesied of "perilous times" in the last days (2 Timothy 3:1), and he warned, "We wrestle not against flesh and blood, but against principalities, against powers, against the rulers of the darkness of this world, against spiritual wickedness in high places" (Ephesians 6:12).

Isaiah promised, "In righteousness shalt thou be established: thou shalt be far from oppression; for thou shalt not fear: and from terror; for it shall not come near thee" (Isaiah 54:14).

The Lord Himself encouraged, "Wherefore, be of good cheer, and do not fear, for I the Lord am with you, and will stand by you; and ye shall bear record of me, even Jesus Christ, that I am the Son of the living God, that I was, that I am, and that I am to come" (D&C 68:6).

The Church

The ward council is the perfect place to establish the balance between home and Church. Here the brethren of the priesthood, themselves fathers, and sisters of the auxiliaries, themselves mothers, can, with inspired insight, coordinate the work of the organizations, each of which serves different members of the family. Here the home and the family can be anchored in place, and the Church can support rather than supplant the parents. Fathers and mothers will understand both their obligation to teach their children and the blessings provided by the Church.

18

A DEFENSE AND A REFUGE

On July 26, 1847, their third day in the valley (the second having been the Sabbath), Brigham Young, with members of the Twelve and some others, climbed a peak about one and a half miles from Temple Square. They thought it a good place to raise an ensign to the nations. Heber C. Kimball wore a yellow bandanna. They tied it to Willard Richards's walking stick and waved it aloft, an ensign to the nations. Brigham Young named it Ensign Peak (see Journal of Wilford Woodruff, 26 July 1847, Church History Library).

Then they descended to their worn-out wagons, to the few things they had carried two thousand miles, and to their travel-weary followers. It was not what they possessed that gave them strength but what they knew.

They knew they were Apostles of the Lord Jesus Christ. They knew that the priesthood had been delivered to them by angelic messengers. They knew they had the commandments and the covenants to offer

From an address given at general conference, October 1, 2006; see *Ensign*, Nov. 2006, 85–88.

opportunity for the eternal salvation and exaltation of all mankind. They were sure that the inspiration of the Holy Ghost attended them.

They busied themselves plowing gardens, putting up shelters against the winter soon to come. They prepared for others already on the prairie following them to this new gathering place.

A revelation, written nine years earlier, directed them to "arise and shine forth, that thy light may be a standard for the nations;

"And that the gathering together upon the land of Zion, and upon her stakes, may be for a defense, and for a refuge from the storm, and from wrath when it shall be poured out without mixture upon the whole earth" (D&C 115:5–6).

They were to be the "light," the "standard."

The standard, established by revelation, is contained in the scriptures through the doctrines of the gospel of Jesus Christ. The principles of the gospel life we follow are based on doctrine, and the standards accord with the principles. We are bound to the standards by covenant, as administered through the ordinances of the gospel by those who have received priesthood and the keys of authority.

Those faithful Brethren were not free, and we are not free, to alter the standards or to ignore them. We must live by them.

It is not a cure or a comfort to simply say they do not matter. We all know they do matter, for all mankind is "instructed sufficiently that they know good from evil" (2 Nephi 2:5).

If we are doing the best we can, we should not become discouraged. When we fall short, as we do, or stumble, which we might, there is always the remedy of repentance and forgiveness.

We are to teach our children the moral standard to avoid every kind of immorality. The precious powers within their mortal bodies "are to be employed only between man and woman, lawfully wedded as husband and wife" ("The Family: A Proclamation to the World," *Ensign*, Nov. 2010, 129). We must be completely faithful in marriage.

We are to keep the law of tithing. We attend to our responsibilities in the Church. We gather each week for sacrament meeting to renew the covenants and earn the promises in those simple and sacred prayers over the bread and water. We are to honor the priesthood and be obedient to the covenants and ordinances.

Those Brethren on Ensign Peak knew that they were to live ordinary lives and keep the image of Christ engraven in their countenances (see Alma 5:14).

They understood that the stakes were to be a defense and a refuge, but at that time there was not one stake on the earth. They knew their mission was to establish stakes of Zion in every nation of the earth.

Perhaps they wondered what kind of wrath or storm could be poured out that they had not already experienced. They had endured savage opposition, violence, terrorism. Their homes had been burned, their property taken. They were driven from their homes time after time after time. They knew then, as we know now, that there would be no end to opposition. The nature of it changes, but it never ends. There would be no end to the kinds of challenges that the early Saints would face. New challenges would be different from, but certainly not less than, those through which they had made their way.

Now the stakes of Zion number in the thousands and are all over the world. The members number in the millions and growing. Neither of these can be held back, for this is the work of the Lord. Now members live in 160 nations and speak over 200 languages.

Some live with an unspoken fear of what awaits us and the Church in the world. It grows ever darker in morality and spirituality. If we will gather into the Church, live the simple principles of the gospel, live moral lives, keep the Word of Wisdom, tend to our priesthood and other duties, then we need not live in fear. The Word of Wisdom is a key to both physical health and revelation. Avoid tea, coffee, liquor, tobacco, and narcotics.

We can live where we wish, doing the best we can to make a living, whether modest or generous. We are free to do as we wish with our lives, assured of the approval and even the intervention of the Almighty, confident of constant spiritual guidance.

Each stake is a defense and a refuge and a standard. A stake is self-contained with all that is needed for the salvation and exaltation of those who would come within its influence, and temples are ever closer.

There has been no end to opposition. There are misinterpretations and misrepresentations of us and of our history, some of it mean-spirited and certainly contrary to the teachings of Jesus Christ and His gospel. Sometimes clergy, even ministerial organizations, oppose us. They do what we would never do. We do not attack or criticize or oppose others as they do us.

Even today there are those preposterous stories handed down and repeated so many times they are believed. One of the silliest of them is that Mormons have horns.

Years ago, I was at a symposium at a college in Oregon. Present were a Catholic bishop, a rabbi, an Episcopalian minister, an Evangelical minister, a Unitarian clergyman, and myself.

The president of the school, Dr. Bennett, hosted a breakfast. One of them asked which wife I had brought. I told them I had a choice of one. For a second, I thought that I was being singled out for embarrassment. Then someone asked the Catholic bishop if he had brought his wife.

The next question came from Dr. Bennett to me: "Is it true that Mormons have horns?"

I smiled and said, "I comb my hair so that they can't be seen."

Dr. Bennett, who was completely bald, put both hands on the top of his head and said, "Oh! You can never make a Mormon out of me!"

Strangest of all, otherwise intelligent people claim we are not Christian. This shows that they know little or nothing about us. It is a true principle that you cannot lift yourself by putting others down.

Some suppose that our high standards will repel growth. It is just the opposite. High standards are a magnet. We are all children of God, drawn to the truth and to good.

We face the challenge of raising families in the world in darkening clouds of wickedness. Some of our members are unsettled, and sometimes they wonder: Is there any place one can go to escape from it all? Is there another town or a state or a country where it is safe, where one can find refuge? The answer generally is no. The defense and the refuge is where our members now live.

The Book of Mormon prophesies, "Yea, and then shall the work commence, with the Father among all nations in preparing the way whereby his people may be gathered home to the land of their inheritance" (3 Nephi 21:28).

Those who come out of the world into the Church, keep the commandments, honor the priesthood, and enter into activity have found the refuge.

In one of our meetings, Elder Robert C. Oaks, then one of the Presidency of the Seventy (a retired four-star general and commander of NATO air forces in Central Europe), reminded us of an accord signed by ten nations on board the battleship *Missouri* in Tokyo Bay on September 2, 1945, which ended World War II. Some of us were in Asia at the time. Said Elder (General) Oaks: "I can't even imagine a circumstance today in which such a meeting could be held or such an accord could be signed to end the war against terrorism and wickedness in which we are engaged. It is not that kind of war."

We are not to be afraid, even in a world where the hostilities will never end. The war of opposition that was prophesied in the revelations continues today. We are to be happy and positive.

All the struggles and exertions of past generations have brought to us in our day the fulness of the gospel of Jesus Christ, the authority to administer, and the wherewithal to accomplish the ministry. It all comes together in this dispensation of the fulness of times, in the which the consummation of all things will be completed and the earth prepared for the coming of the Lord.

We are as much a part of this work as were those men who untied that yellow bandanna from Willard Richards's walking stick and descended from Ensign Peak. That bandanna, waved aloft, signaled the great gathering which had been prophesied in ancient and modern scriptures.

We speak of the Church as our refuge, our defense. There is safety and protection in the Church. It centers in the gospel of Jesus Christ. Latter-day Saints learn to look within themselves to see the redeeming power of the Savior of all mankind. The principles of the gospel taught in the Church and learned from the scriptures become a guide for each of us individually and for our families.

We know that the homes we establish, and those of our descendants, will be the refuge spoken of in the revelations—the "light," the "standard," the "ensign" for all nations, and the "refuge" against the gathering storms (see D&C 115:5–6; Isaiah 11:12; 2 Nephi 21:12).

The ensign to which all of us are to rally is Jesus Christ, the Son of God, the Only Begotten of the Father, whose Church this is and whose name we bear and whose authority we carry.

We look forward with faith. We have seen many events in our lifetime, and many will yet occur that will tax our courage and extend our faith. We are to "rejoice, and be exceeding glad: for great [will be our] reward in heaven" (Matthew 5:12).

Willingly defend the history of the Church, and do "not [be] ashamed of the gospel of [Jesus] Christ: for it is the power of God unto salvation to every one that believeth" (Romans 1:16). We will face the challenges, for we cannot avoid them, and teach the gospel of Jesus Christ and teach of Him as our Savior and our Refuge, our Redeemer.

If a well-worn yellow bandanna was good enough to be an ensign to the world, then ordinary men who hold the priesthood and ordinary women and ordinary children in ordinary families, living the gospel as best they can all over the world, can shine forth as a standard, a defense, a refuge against whatever is to be poured out upon the earth.

"We talk of Christ, we rejoice in Christ, we preach of Christ, we prophesy of Christ, and we write according to our prophecies, that our children may know to what source they may look for a remission of their sins" (2 Nephi 25:26).

This Church will prosper. It will prevail. Of this I am absolutely certain.

19

THE STANDARD OF TRUTH HAS BEEN ERECTED

It is my purpose to explain to the youth and young adults, and to their parents, why we hold so rigidly to high standards of moral conduct; why we avoid addictive drugs and tea, coffee, alcohol, and tobacco; why we teach standards of modesty in dress, grooming, and speech (see *For the Strength of Youth* [pamphlet, 2001]). You need to know where our standards came from and why we cannot loosen up and follow what the world does.

You have your agency—"moral agency" (D&C 101:78). You are free to choose your standards.

You will understand better if I speak of scripture and doctrine rather than about behavior.

The Church you belong to, The Church of Jesus Christ of Latter-day Saints, is the restored Church (see D&C 115:4). When you know what *restored* means, you will understand why standards of conduct are as they are.

From an address given at general conference, October 4, 2003; see *Ensign,* Nov. 2003, 24–27.

156

Following the Crucifixion of Christ an apostasy occurred. Leaders began to "teach for doctrines the commandments of men" (Joseph Smith—History 1:19). They lost the keys of authority and closed themselves off from the channels of revelation. That lost authority could not just be repossessed. It had to be restored by those who held the keys of authority anciently (see D&C 27:12–13).

The Church of Jesus Christ of Latter-day Saints is not a remodeled version of another church. It is not an adjustment or a correction or a protest against any other church. They have their "form of godliness" (Joseph Smith—History 1:19) and their goodness and value.

John the Baptist returned through the veil to confer the Aaronic Priesthood, "which holds the keys of the ministering of angels, and of the gospel of repentance, and of baptism by immersion for the remission of sins" (D&C 13:1). A companion ordinance, confirmation and the conferral of the gift of the Holy Ghost, required a greater authority (see D&C 20:41; 33:15).

Soon thereafter, Peter, James, and John, Apostle companions of the Lord, restored the higher or Melchizedek Priesthood (see D&C 27:12–13; Joseph Smith—History 1:72)—"the Holy Priesthood, after the Order of the Son of God" (D&C 107:3).

The Restoration did not come all at once. In a series of visitations, other prophets came to restore the keys of the priesthood (see D&C 110).

With the authority restored, the organization was revealed. Apostles were ordained, and the Quorum of the Twelve Apostles and First Presidency were organized as they had been anciently (see D&C 18:9; 20:1–2; 107:22, 29). The ordinances were revealed and authority given to perform them.

The Book of Mormon: Another Testament of Jesus Christ was translated and published. In it is "the fulness of [the] everlasting gospel" (D&C 27:5).

Other revelations were published—the Doctrine and Covenants

and the Pearl of Great Price. From those books of scripture, we learned why the earth was created and who created it (see Moses 1:30–39). There was opened to the early leaders of the Church the fulness of the gospel of Jesus Christ and the *standards* He requires of His disciples.

We learned about the plan of redemption—"the great plan of happiness" (Alma 42:8). We came to earth to be tested and to gain experience, with a promise that "through the Atonement of Christ, all mankind may be saved, by obedience to the laws and ordinances of the Gospel" (Articles of Faith 1:3).

The great plan of happiness enables family relationships to last beyond the grave. Sacred ordinances and covenants, available only in the temple, make it possible for individuals to return to the presence of God and for families to be united eternally. Marriage, the family, and the home are the foundation of the Church. Nothing is more important to the Church and to civilization itself than the family!

For some all is not complete in mortal life, for marriage and a family of their own have passed them by. But the great plan of happiness and the laws which govern it continue after death. Watched over by a kind and loving Heavenly Father, they will not, in the eternal pattern of things, be denied blessings necessary for their exaltation, including marriage and family. And it will be sweeter still because of the waiting and the longing.

We learned from the revelations that we do not have to tell you young people what is right and what is wrong with regard to morality and marriage. The prophet Lehi taught his youthful children that "men are instructed sufficiently that they know good from evil" (2 Nephi 2:5).

Because the power to create a mortal body is essential to our happiness and exaltation, the Lord has decreed severe penalties against the immoral use of that power to beget life (see Jacob 3:12; D&C 42:24; 104:8–9). Satan knows that if he can corrupt the process of mating and cause men and women to degrade it in immoral acts, he will, to that degree, for them disrupt the plan of happiness.

Paul taught, "God . . . will not suffer you to be tempted above that ye are able; but will with the temptation also make a way to escape, that ye may be able to bear it" (1 Corinthians 10:13).

I do not wish to offend the delicate feelings of you wonderful young people, but in your world awash with iniquity, you must be on guard.

There are words we would rather not say. They describe things that we would rather not think about. But you are inescapably exposed to temptations in connection with fornication, adultery, pornography, prostitution, perversion, lust, abuse, the unnatural, and all that grows from them.

Only with difficulty can you escape the degrading profanity and wicked, joking humor that accompanies them. It is all paraded before you in unworthy entertainment—music, print, drama, film, television, and, of course, the Internet.

Remember the First Vision when young Joseph knelt in the grove. Immediately thick darkness gathered around him. He was seized by the power of the enemy, an actual being from the unseen world. He did what every one of you can do. He called upon God, and the evil power left him (see Joseph Smith—History 1:15–16).

There is great power in prayer. As a son or a daughter of God, you can, as Joseph did, pray to God in the name of Jesus Christ for strength (see James 4:7).

Satan, with his angels, will try to capture your thoughts and control what you do. If he can, he will corrupt anything that is good (see D&C 10:22). To him the Internet is just that—a net to ensnare you into wicked addiction with pornography. Unhappiness will follow (see Alma 41:10).

Some work through political, social, and legal channels to redefine morality and marriage into something unrestrained, unnatural, and forbidden. But they never can change the design which has governed human life and happiness from the beginning. The deceiver preys upon some passion or tendency or weakness. He convinces them that the condition cannot be changed and recruits them for activities for which they never would volunteer.

But sooner or later that spark of divinity in each of them will ignite. They can assert their agency as sons and daughters created in the image of God (see Genesis 1:26–27; Moses 2:26–27; 6:9; Abraham 4:26–27) and renounce the destroyer. That which they had been led to believe could not be changed, will be changed, and they will feel the power of the redemption of Christ (see 2 Nephi 2:1–6). Their burden will be lifted and the pain healed up (see Alma 7:11–12). That is what the Atonement of Christ is all about.

They can claim their inheritance as children of heavenly parents and, despite the tortured, agonizing test of mortal life, know that they are not lost.

In the Church, one is not condemned for tendencies or temptations. One is held accountable for transgression (see D&C 101:78; Articles of Faith 1:2). If you do not act on unworthy persuasions, you will neither be condemned nor be subject to Church discipline.

We do not set the standards, but we are commanded to teach them and maintain them. The standard remains abstinence before marriage and total fidelity in marriage. However out of step we may seem, however much the standards are belittled, however much others yield, we will not yield, we cannot yield. Obedience to the moral standard and observance of the Word of Wisdom will remain as requirements for ordination to the priesthood, for a mission, and for a temple recommend.

You had conferred upon you the gift of the Holy Ghost. There will be whisperings of approval or warning when you have decisions to make (see D&C 8:2–3; 9:7–9). The Holy Ghost can guide you away from evil and bring you back if you have wandered and lost your path. Never forget that you are sons and daughters of God. Satan cannot forever imprison you. You always hold the key of repentance to unlock the prison door.

If you, our youth, feel alone, remember there are millions of you in the Church now. Tens of thousands of you at this moment serve missions. You are a visible example, a testimony of the Restoration, even to those who will not listen to your message. Wherever you are—in school, at work or play, in the military—you are never alone.

Now, words can be used as weapons against you. If they throw the word *diversity* at you, grab hold of it and say, "I am already diverse, and I intend to stay diverse." If the word is *tolerance*, grab that one too, saying, "I expect you to be tolerant of my lifestyle—obedience, integrity, abstinence, repentance." If the word is *choice*, tell them you choose good, old-fashioned morality. You choose to be a worthy husband or wife, a worthy parent.

The whole Church may stand alone in defense of these standards. But we are not the first. Moroni, the last of his people, said: "I even remain alone. . . . I fulfil the commandment of my father" (Mormon 8:3). Do not be afraid (see 2 Timothy 1:7; D&C 68:6).

When I was young and very new in my calling, I was sent east to meet with powerful, prominent officials who were blocking our work. As I left for the airport, I stopped to see President Harold B. Lee and asked, "Do you have any parting counsel?"

"Yes," he said, "just remember this isn't 1830, and there aren't just six of us."

That erased fear. I pled our cause. The problem was resolved.

Society is on a course that has caused the destruction of civilizations and is now ripening in iniquity. Civilization itself is at stake. You, our wonderful youth, are an example to untold millions of good people worldwide.

I think of the joy and happiness that await you in this life and the work you are to do, and I cannot be discouraged. Peter, the Apostle who stood next to the Lord, said of you, "Ye are a chosen generation, a royal priesthood, an holy nation, a peculiar people; that ye should shew forth the praises of him who hath called you out of darkness into his marvellous light" (1 Peter 2:9).

Remember this great prophecy:

"The Standard of Truth has been erected; no unhallowed hand can stop the work from progressing; . . . the truth of God will go forth boldly, nobly, and independent, till it has penetrated every continent, visited every clime, swept every country, and sounded in every ear, till the purposes of God shall be accomplished, and the Great Jehovah shall say the work is done" (Joseph Smith, *History of The Church of Jesus Christ of Latter-day Saints,* 7 vols. [1932–1951], 4:540).

> *Shall the youth of Zion falter*
> *In defending truth and right?*
> *While the enemy assaileth,*
> *Shall we shrink or shun the fight? No!*
> *True to the faith that our parents have cherished,*
> *True to the truth for which martyrs have perished,*
> *To God's command, Soul, heart, and hand,*
> *Faithful and true we will ever stand.*
>
> *While we know the pow'rs of darkness*
> *Seek to thwart the work of God,*
> *Shall the children of the promise*
> *Cease to grasp the iron rod? No! . . .*
>
> *We will work out our salvation;*
> *We will cleave unto the truth;*
> *We will watch and pray and labor*
> *With the fervent zeal of youth. Yes! . . .*
>
> *We will strive to be found worthy*
> *Of the kingdom of our Lord,*
> *With the faithful ones redeemed*
> *Who have loved and kept his word. Yes! . . .*

True to the faith that our parents have cherished,
True to the truth for which martyrs have perished,
To God's command, Soul, heart and hand,
Faithful and true we will ever stand.
("True to the Faith," *Hymns*, no. 254)

God bless you millions of youth in our Church who worthily follow the patterns of the gospel and have within you a deep testimony—the testimony that all of us share and bear.

20

ON ZION'S HILL

I have lived a long time and watched the standards upon which civilization must depend for survival be swept aside one piece at a time.

We live in a day when the age-old standards of morality, marriage, home, and family suffer defeat after defeat in courts and councils, in parliaments and classrooms. Our happiness depends upon living those very standards.

The Apostle Paul prophesied that in our day, these last days, men would be "disobedient to parents, . . . without natural affection, . . . despisers of those that are good, . . . lovers of pleasures more than lovers of God" (2 Timothy 3:2–4).

And he warned: "Evil men and seducers shall wax worse and worse, deceiving, and being deceived" (2 Timothy 3:13). He was right. Nevertheless, when I think of the future, I am overwhelmed with a feeling of positive optimism.

Paul told young Timothy to continue in the things he had learned

From an address given at general conference, October 2, 2005; see *Ensign,* November 2005, 70–73.

from the Apostles and said he would be safe because "from a child thou hast known the holy scriptures, which are able to make thee wise unto salvation through faith which is in Christ Jesus" (2 Timothy 3:15). A knowledge of the scriptures is important. From them we learn about spiritual guidance.

I have heard people say, "I would have willingly endured persecution and trials if I might have lived in the early years of the Church when there was such a flow of revelation published as scripture. Why is that not happening now?"

The revelations that came through the Prophet Joseph Smith, printed as scripture, laid the permanent foundation of the Church through which the gospel of Jesus Christ could go forth to "every nation" (2 Nephi 26:13; see also Revelation 5:9; 14:6; 1 Nephi 19:17; Mosiah 3:13, 20; 15:28; 16:1; Alma 9:20; 37:4; D&C 10:51; 77:8, 11; 133:37).

The scriptures define the office of the Prophet and President and his Counselors, the Quorum of the Twelve Apostles, quorums of the Seventy, the Presiding Bishopric, and the stakes and wards and branches. They define the offices of the Melchizedek and Aaronic Priesthoods. They establish the channels through which inspiration and revelation can flow to the leaders and teachers and parents and to individuals.

The opposition and trials are different now. If anything, they are more intense, more dangerous than in those early days, aimed not so much at the Church as at us as individuals. The early revelations, published as scriptures for the permanent guidance of the Church, define the ordinances and covenants and are still in force.

One of those scriptures promises, "If ye are prepared ye shall not fear" (D&C 38:30).

Let me tell you what has been done to prepare us. Perhaps you will then understand why I do not fear the future, why I have such positive feelings of confidence.

165

I cannot possibly describe in detail or even list all that has been put in place by the First Presidency and the Quorum of the Twelve Apostles in recent years. In them you will see continuing revelation, open to the Church and to each individual member. I will describe a few of them.

More than forty years ago, it was determined to make the doctrine quickly and easily available to every member of the Church by preparing a Latter-day Saint edition of the scriptures. We set out to cross-reference the King James Bible with the Book of Mormon, the Doctrine and Covenants, and the Pearl of Great Price. The text of the King James Bible was left completely unaltered.

Work was done centuries ago to prepare for our day. Ninety percent of the King James Bible is as translated by William Tyndale and John Wycliffe. We owe much to those early translators, those martyrs.

William Tyndale said, "I will cause a boy that driveth the plough shall know more of the Scripture than [the clergy]" (in David Danielle, introduction to *Tyndale's New Testament,* trans. by William Tyndale [1989], viii).

The Book of Mormon prophet Alma had come through great trials and faced even greater ones. And the record says, "And now, as the preaching of the word had a great tendency to lead the people to do that which was just—yea, it had had more powerful effect upon the minds of the people than the sword, or anything else, which had happened unto them—therefore Alma thought it was expedient that they should try the virtue of the word of God" (Alma 31:5).

That is exactly what we had in mind when we began the scripture project: that every member of the Church could know the scriptures and understand the principles and doctrines to be found in them. We set out to do in our day what Tyndale and Wycliffe had done in theirs.

Both Tyndale and Wycliffe were terribly persecuted. Tyndale suffered in a freezing prison in Brussels. His clothing was worn to rags, and he was terribly cold. He wrote to the bishops asking for his coat and cap. He begged for a candle, saying, "It is indeed wearisome sitting alone in the dark" (in Danielle, introduction to *Tyndale's New Testament,* ix). They were so enraged at this request that he was taken from prison and, before a large crowd, strangled and then burned at the stake.

Wycliffe escaped death by burning, but the Council of Constance had his body exhumed, burned at the stake, and his ashes scattered (see John Foxe, *Foxe's Book of Martyrs,* ed. G. A. Williamson [1965], 18–20).

The Prophet Joseph Smith had borrowed the volumes of the *Book of Martyrs* by the sixteenth-century English cleric John Foxe from the mother of Edward Stevenson of the Seventy. After he read them, he said, "I have, by the aid of the Urim and Thummim, seen those martyrs, and they were honest, devoted followers of Christ, according to the light they possessed, and they will be saved" (in Edward Stevenson, *Reminiscences of Joseph, the Prophet, and the Coming Forth of the Book of Mormon* [1893], 6).

To cross-reference more than 70,000 verses of scripture and provide footnotes and helps was known to be enormously difficult, perhaps even impossible. But it was begun. It took twelve years and the help of more than six hundred people to complete. Some were experts in Greek, Latin, and Hebrew or had a knowledge of ancient scriptures. But most were ordinary, faithful members of the Church.

The spirit of inspiration brooded over the work.

The project would have been impossible without the computer.

A remarkable system was designed to organize tens of thousands of footnotes to open the scriptures to every ploughboy and every ploughgirl.

With a subject-matter index, a member can, in just a few minutes, look up such words as *atonement, repentance,* and *Holy Ghost* and find revealing references from all four scriptures.

Several years into the project, we asked how they were progressing with the tedious, laborious listing of topics in alphabetical order. They wrote, "We have been through *Heaven* and *Hell,* past *Love* and *Lust,* and now we're working toward *Repentance.*"

Original manuscripts of the Book of Mormon came into our hands. These made possible the correction of printers' errors which creep into scriptural translations.

Most notable in the Topical Guide are the eighteen pages, single-spaced, small print, under the heading "Jesus Christ," the most comprehensive compilation of scriptural information on the name Jesus Christ that has ever been assembled in the history of the world. Follow these references, and you will open the door to whose Church this is, what it teaches and by what authority, all anchored to the sacred name of Jesus Christ, the Son of God, the Messiah, the Redeemer, our Lord.

Two new revelations were added to the Doctrine and Covenants—section 137, a vision given to Joseph Smith the Prophet on the occasion of the administration of the endowment, and section 138, President Joseph F. Smith's vision of the redemption of the dead. Then, just as this work was being closed for printing, the marvelous revelation on the priesthood was received and announced in an official declaration (see D&C Official Declaration 2), proving that the scriptures are not closed.

Then came the enormous challenge of translation into the languages of the Church. Now the triple combination has been published in more than two dozen languages, with others to follow. The Book of Mormon is now printed in more than a hundred languages. Many additional translations are under way.

Other things were done. The Book of Mormon was given a subtitle—The Book of Mormon: Another Testament of Jesus Christ.

With the foundation doctrines in place as solid as the granite in the Salt Lake Temple and open to everyone, more people could witness the constant flow of revelation to the Church. "We believe all that God has revealed, all that He does now reveal, and we believe that He will yet reveal many great and important things pertaining to the Kingdom of God" (Articles of Faith 1:9).

While the scripture publication moved on, another great work was begun. This too would take years. The entire curriculum of the Church was restructured. All courses of study in priesthood and auxiliary organizations—for children, youth, and adults—were revised to center on the scriptures, to center on Jesus Christ, to center on the priesthood, and to center on the family.

Hundreds of volunteers worked year in and year out. Some of them were experts in writing, curriculum, instruction, and other related fields, but most were ordinary members of the Church. It was all anchored in the scriptures, with emphasis on the authority of the priesthood and with focus on the sacred nature of the family.

The First Presidency and the Quorum of the Twelve Apostles issued "The Family: A Proclamation to the World" (*Ensign,* Nov. 1995, 102). They then published "The Living Christ: The Testimony of the Apostles" (*Ensign,* Apr. 2000, 2).

Seminaries and institutes of religion spread across the world. The teachers and students learn and teach by the Spirit (see D&C 50:17–22), and both are taught to understand the scriptures, the words of the prophets, the plan of salvation, the Atonement of Jesus Christ, the Apostasy and Restoration, and the unique position of the restored Church, and to identify the principles and doctrines found in them. Students are encouraged to develop a habit of daily scripture study.

Monday night was reserved for family home evening. All activities of the Church are to yield so that families can be together.

In natural sequence, missionary work was reanchored to the revelations under the title "Preach My Gospel." Each year more than 25,000 missionaries are released to return to their homes in 148 countries, after spending two years learning the doctrine and how to teach by the Spirit and sharing their testimonies.

Principles of priesthood government have been clarified. The place of the quorums of the priesthood—Aaronic and Melchizedek—has been magnified. Always, everywhere, there are leaders who hold the keys—bishops and presidents—to give guidance, to clarify misunderstandings, to detect and correct false doctrines.

The course of study for adults in Priesthood and Relief Society is based on the teachings of the Presidents of the Church.

Church magazines have been redesigned and are published now in fifty languages.

An awesome era of temple building goes on.

Genealogy was renamed "Family History." Faithful members are aided by the newest technology to prepare and bring names to the temple.

These things all witness of continuing revelation. There are other things, too numerous to describe in detail.

There is in the Church a central core of power deeper than programs or meetings or associations. It does not change. It cannot erode. It is constant and certain. It never recedes or fades.

While the Church is housed in chapels, it lives in the heart and soul of every Latter-day Saint.

Everywhere in the world, humble members draw inspiration from the scriptures to guide them through life, not fully understanding that they have found that "pearl of great price" (Matthew 13:46) about which the Lord spoke to His disciples.

When Emma Smith, wife of the Prophet Joseph, collected hymns for the first hymnbook, she included "Guide Us, O Thou Great Jehovah," which is, in fact, a prayer:

> *When the earth begins to tremble,*
> *Bid our fearful thoughts be still;*
> *When thy judgments spread destruction,*
> *Keep us safe on Zion's hill.*
> ("Guide Us, O Thou Great Jehovah,"
> *Hymns,* no. 83)

Every soul who willingly affiliates with The Church of Jesus Christ of Latter-day Saints and seeks to abide by its principles and ordinances is standing "on Zion's hill."

Each can receive assurance which comes through inspiration and testifies that Jesus is the Christ, the Son of God, that The Church of Jesus Christ of Latter-day Saints is just as He declared it to be, "the only true and living church upon the face of the whole earth" (D&C 1:30).

21

THE GATHERING

From the Old Testament to the modern revelations, the scriptures are laced with references to the words *gather* and *gathering*.

The first gathering came early in this the dispensation of the fulness of times. It was to Kirtland, Ohio. There the Saints built a temple. There Joseph Smith and Oliver Cowdery "saw the Lord standing upon the breastwork of the pulpit," and He prophesied to them that the work would go forth until it filled the whole earth, and "the fame of this house shall spread to foreign lands" (D&C 110:2, 10).

Then Moses appeared "and committed unto us the keys of the *gathering* of Israel from the four parts of the earth"—the *gathering*, the *keys*—"and the leading of the ten tribes from the land of the north" (D&C 110:11; emphasis added).

Elias "committed the dispensation of the gospel of Abraham," promising that "in us and our seed all generations after us should be blessed" (D&C 110:12).

From an address given at the seminar for new mission presidents, 2006.

172

And then "another great and glorious vision burst upon [them]; for Elijah the prophet, who was taken to heaven without tasting death, stood before [them]" and announced "[the turning of] the hearts of the fathers to the children, and the children to the fathers" and said, "Therefore, the keys of this dispensation are committed into your hands; and by this ye may know that the great and dreadful day of the Lord is near, even at the doors" (D&C 110:13, 15–16).

Those keys of gathering were given then and remain in the Church today.

The Saints were driven away from Kirtland and gathered at Independence, Missouri. There they laid the cornerstones for another temple. Again they were driven away to Far West, Missouri.

In 1838 at Far West, the Lord revealed the name of the Church: "For thus shall my church be called in the last days, even The Church of Jesus Christ of Latter-day Saints. . . .

"And that the gathering together upon the land of Zion, and upon her stakes, may be for a defense, and for a refuge from the storm, and from wrath when it shall be poured out without mixture upon the whole earth" (D&C 115:4, 6).

They were commanded to build a temple at Far West, but they were not to see it built. The mobs drove them away. The Twelve went back at night to set the cornerstones. Wilford Woodruff was ordained an Apostle sitting on one of those cornerstones.

Then they were driven east to Nauvoo, Illinois. They built the city and the temple. The call went out to gather at Nauvoo, and they came.

When we arrived in New England in 1965 to preside over the mission, there was one small branch in Dartmouth, Nova Scotia, across the river from Halifax. A small chapel had recently been built. I was surprised to learn that in Halifax there had been a branch of three hundred people in the early days of the Church. When the signal came to gather to Nauvoo, all of them left. We started over again to build up the Church.

173

The first time the restored gospel was preached on the islands of the sea was on the Fox Islands off the coast of Maine, now called Vinalhaven. Wilford Woodruff walked ten miles to Portland, Maine, then boarded a sloop which took him over to the islands. (As I remember, they are about ten or twelve miles up the coast.) Elder Woodruff evidently went there alone.

He recorded: "The first two we baptized were a sea-captain, by the name of Justin Eames, and his wife. . . . These were the first baptisms performed by proper authority upon any of the islands of the sea . . . in this dispensation" (Matthias F. Cowley, *Wilford Woodruff: History of His Life and Labors* [1964], 78). He recorded, as well, that he had to chop the block ice out of the inlet in order to have open water for the baptism.

About that time, a letter arrived from President Thomas B. Marsh of the Quorum of the Twelve Apostles. In it was recorded a revelation which is now the 118th section of the Doctrine and Covenants. John Taylor, John E. Page, Wilford Woodruff, and Willard Richards were called to the Quorum of the Twelve. Elder Woodruff said, "The substance of this letter had been revealed to me several weeks before, but I had not named it to any person" (Ibid., 93).

He continued his missionary work in earnest. It was not easy. There is one account of him going to a meeting in which he said, "We wallowed through snowdrifts . . . to meet an appointment to preach in a schoolhouse, and on the way I got one of my ears frozen. [We met] a large and attentive audience" (Ibid., 84–85).

Elder Woodruff said of two other missionaries: "After laboring upon the island for about four weeks, Elder Hyde was taken with a violent attack of typhus fever. He was confined to his bed for about nine weeks and it seemed that death was determined to conquer. But through the goodness of God his life was spared. Elder Herritt waited upon him with great fidelity when he was not called away to fill appointments. On the 10th of October, [Elder Herritt] too was taken sick with the disease. Elder Herritt seemed to know from the first that it was not the will of the Lord that he should recover and died October 19, 1840." He had so reduced his energies and his capacities in taking care of his sick companion and meeting all the appointments, he was worn down so he did not have the resistance to fight the disease. Elder Hyde wrote, "'Elder Herritt was a good man and was willing to wade through all kinds of opposition for the truth's sake, and whenever he could get the privilege of standing before the congregations of the wicked to declare the truths of the Gospel, although opposition might rage, he was at the height of his glory. Our hearts were knit together as were the hearts of David and Jonathan.'

"During the sickness of Elder Hyde, Elder Herritt baptized three persons. After the death of Elder Herritt, Elder Hyde, although only 22 years of age, and performing his first mission, continued his labors [alone]" ("History of New England Mission," private publication, 59).

Then came the call for the Saints on the Fox Islands to gather at Nauvoo.

They left Maine on October 4, 1838, crossing part of Maine, New Hampshire, Vermont, and part of New York. They traveled with horses and wagons. Wilford Woodruff said there were problems. "Those men were all fishermen," he said. "They were more acquainted with sharks than they were with horses" (see Cowley, *Wilford Woodruff*, 94). But the call to gather had come. They suffered intensely.

The weather turned bad; it rained and then snowed. Wilford Woodruff's wife was very ill. She grew sicker by the day. Finally, it was apparent that she would not live. They stopped at a house. It was raining and cold and miserable. He picked his wife up from the wagon, carried her to the door, and put his foot against the door and pushed it open forcefully. He said he did not wait to be admitted for fear they would be turned away. He was determined that his wife would not die outdoors.

She lingered for a few hours, and then she died. And then it happened! Wilford Woodruff recorded that for the first time during her sickness his heart was filled with faith, and he blessed his wife to return to life. Miraculously, she revived. She recounted how marvelous it was beyond the veil, yet she yearned to come back. Consent was given on the condition that she would follow her husband through all that he would be called to do in mortality (see ibid., 96–98).

There was a similar incident with President Marion G. Romney. I remember that his wife, Ida, was very low, very ill, and it was thought that her life would soon be over. He told me the same thing that Elder Woodruff had said. He said, "For the first time, my heart was filled with great faith." He administered to her, and she lived.

The Saints from the Fox Islands finally arrived at Quincy, Illinois, on April 18, 1839, after six months of intense trials and suffering—one of the great epics in Church history.

In time, persecution at Nauvoo became intense. The Saints left their homes and farms and shops, heading west into the wilderness to gather in a land no one had seen except in vision.

The prophecy of Isaiah was to be fulfilled: "And it shall come to pass in the last days, that the mountain of the Lord's house shall be established in the top of the mountains, and shall be exalted above the hills; and all nations shall flow unto it.

"And many people shall go and say, Come ye, and let us go up to the mountain of the Lord, to the house of the God of Jacob; and he will teach us of his ways, and we will walk in his paths: for out of Zion shall go forth the law, and the word of the Lord from Jerusalem" (Isaiah 2:2–3).

Jeremiah had also prophesied: "And I will gather the remnant of my flock out of all countries whither I have driven them, and will bring them again to their folds; and they shall be fruitful and increase" (Jeremiah 23:3).

Again the Saints were commanded to build the Lord's house.

The call had already gone out some years earlier to members scattered abroad to gather to Zion. The First Presidency of the Church had sent a declaration entitled, "A Proclamation of the First Presidency of the Church to the Saints Scattered Abroad." It was a proclamation of gathering dated January 15, 1841, and was signed by Joseph Smith, Sidney Rigdon, and Hyrum Smith (*History of The Church of Jesus Christ of Latter-day Saints,* 7 vols. [1932–1951], 4:267–73).

The proclamation carried this quotation from the 50th Psalm: "The mighty God, even the Lord, hath spoken. . . . Gather my saints together unto me; those that have made a covenant with me" (Psalm 50:1, 5; see *History of the Church,* 4:272).

The proclamation also told them "they must not expect perfection, or that all will be harmony, peace, and love" (*History of the Church,* 4:272).

About that time, Eliza R. Snow wrote:

> *Think not when you gather to Zion,*
> *The Saints here have nothing to do*
> *But to look to your personal welfare,*
> *And always be comforting you.*
> *No; those who are faithful are doing*
> *What they find to do with their might;*
> *To gather the scattered of Israel*
> *They labor by day and by night.*
>
> *Think not when you gather to Zion,*
> *The prize and the victory won.*
> *Think not that the warfare is ended,*
> *The work of salvation is done.*
> *No, no; for the great prince of darkness*
> *A tenfold exertion will make,*
> *When he sees you go to the fountain,*
> *Where freely the truth you may take.*
> ("Think Not, When You Gather to Zion,"
> *Hymns* [1948], no. 21, vv. 3–4)

The spirit of gathering rested upon them. And they came, first as a trickle, and then as a stream. The Zion to which they came was again under terrible persecution. It was greatly strengthened by their very numbers.

They came across the ocean and prairies and across the wilderness. They climbed over and through the mighty, towering Rocky Mountains. They came by wagon with ox teams. Most all who came walked two thousand miles. Three thousand of them pushed handcarts. The spirit of gathering was in their hearts. The Perpetual Emigration Fund was established to help the poor gather from Europe.

Old Brother Andrews, who lived across the street from us in Brigham City, explained the spirit of gathering in very simple terms: "When you was over there, you wants to come over 'ere."

In 1969 I was supervising Western Europe, assisting Elder Marion G. Romney of the Quorum of the Twelve. The spirit of gathering had been strong for generations. I found that when someone was converted, they wanted to gather to Utah, to Zion.

One day I said to Elder Romney, "If I do as I feel, I will tell them all to stay there."

He said, "I have the same feeling, but I had better talk that over with the Brethren in the temple," and this he did. When he came from the next temple meeting, he said, "The Brethren are in agreement. Tell them to stay where they are."

So I went across Europe preaching, "Stay where you are."

The first time I went to Russia, the same thing was taking place. A convert, soon filled with the spirit of gathering, would want to join the body of the Church in America. The leadership was being drained off again.

Then in August of 1972, quite unnoticed, an historic change was announced, a redirection from the Lord. Gathering was not to continue as it had for nearly 150 years. In an area conference held in Mexico City, Elder Bruce R. McConkie, quoting Jacob, said that the people "shall be gathered home to the lands of their inheritance, and shall be established in all their lands of promise" (2 Nephi 9:2).

Then Elder McConkie said: "The place of gathering for the Mexican Saints is in Mexico; the place of gathering for the Guatemalan Saints is in Guatemala; the place of gathering for the Brazilian Saints is in Brazil; and so it goes throughout the length and breadth of the whole earth. Japan is for the Japanese; Korea is for the Koreans; Australia is for the Australians; *every nation is the gathering place for its own people.*"

He continued: "The Book of Mormon teaching is, 'There is one God and one Shepherd over all the earth. And the time cometh that he shall manifest himself unto all nations.' (1 Nephi 13:41–42.) The gospel is the same everywhere. It does not matter where we live if we keep the commandments of God, and the commandments are the same in all nations and among all people" (in Mexico and Central America Area General Conference Report, Aug. 1972, 45; emphasis added).

Henceforth, they were to be gathered out of the world into the Church in their own lands into the stakes of Zion. A stake is a refuge from the world.

At the next April general conference, the prophet-President of the Church, Harold B. Lee, in effect announced that the pioneering phase of gathering to Utah was now over. To quote President Lee: "We have also been promised by the Lord: 'Behold, and lo, I will take care of your flocks, and will raise up elders and send unto them. Behold, I will hasten my work in its time.' (D&C 88:72–73.)

"Today we are witnessing the demonstration of the Lord's hand even in the midst of his saints, the members of the Church. Never in this dispensation, and perhaps never before in any single period, has there been such a feeling of urgency among the members of this church as today. Her boundaries are being enlarged, her stakes are being strengthened. . . ."

After quoting from Elder McConkie's address in Mexico City, President Lee concluded, "[This] certainly emphasizes the great need for the teaching and training of local leadership in order to build up the church within their own native countries" (in Conference Report, Apr. 1973, 6–7).

A new direction had now been given to the spirit of gathering. The gathering no longer was to be to the tops of the mountains. Under the direction of the apostles and prophets, the gathering was to be out of the world into the Church in every nation. Every nation was to be the gathering place for its own people. They would gather to build temples. It is clear then that the stakes are to be the gathering places and the places of refuge for the members of the Church.

The Prophet Joseph Smith said, "What was the object of gathering . . . the people of God in any age of the world? . . . The main object was to build unto the Lord a house whereby He could reveal unto His people the ordinances of His house and the glories of His kingdom, and teach the people the way of salvation" (*History of the Church,* 5:423).

And that is what missionaries are about today—gathering out of the world the pure in heart to the refuge of the stakes of Zion.

Temple work is centered in families. The ultimate end of all we do in the Church is to see that parents and children are happy at home and sealed together in the temple.

When the revelation was given on baptism for the dead, the Lord said, "It is ordained that in Zion, and in her stakes, . . . those places which I have appointed for refuge, shall be the places for your baptisms for your dead" (D&C 124:36).

For years that bothered me. Baptisms for the dead are to be in temples, but then there were very few temples in the stakes. But now temples are now all over the world, and the temple building goes on.

Mormon said, "Then shall they know their Redeemer, who is Jesus Christ, the Son of God; and then shall they be gathered in from the four quarters of the earth unto their own lands, from whence they have been dispersed; yea, as the Lord liveth so shall it be" (3 Nephi 5:26).

Paul wrote to the Ephesians, "That in the dispensation of the fulness of times he might gather together in one all things in Christ, both which are in heaven, and which are on earth" (Ephesians 1:10).

Threaded through the scriptures—the Old Testament, the New Testament, the Book of Mormon, the Doctrine and Covenants, and the Pearl of Great Price—is that recurring theme of gathering.

All of us in the Church are gatherers, particularly those who serve as missionaries. Those who are in the mission field may sometimes feel the same frustration and desire as the prophet Alma felt:

"O that I were an angel, and could have the wish of mine heart, that I might go forth and speak with the trump of God, with a voice to shake the earth, and cry repentance unto every people!"

Then Alma said, "But behold, I am a man, and do sin in my wish; . . .

"For behold, the Lord doth grant unto all nations, of their own nation and tongue, to teach his word, yea, in wisdom, all that he seeth fit that they should have" (Alma 29:1, 3, 8).

Section 90 of the Doctrine and Covenants, given at Kirtland in 1833, says, "For it shall come to pass in that day, that every man shall hear the fulness of the gospel in his own tongue, and in his own language, through those who are ordained unto this power, by the administration of the Comforter, shed forth upon them for the revelation of Jesus Christ" (D&C 90:11).

Every week one of the Twelve, and sometimes one of the First Presidency, speaks to multiple stakes across the earth and those messages are given in every language through the instrument of faithful and inspired interpreters.

When the Melchizedek Priesthood was restored and Joseph Smith and Oliver Cowdery were ordained to be Apostles by Peter, James, and John, the Lord said:

"I have ordained you and confirmed you to be apostles, and

especial witnesses of my name, and bear the keys of your ministry and of the same things which I revealed unto them;

"Unto whom I have committed the keys of my kingdom, and a dispensation of the gospel for the last times; and for the fulness of times, in the which I will *gather together* in one all things, both which are in heaven, and which are on earth" (D&C 27:12–13; emphasis added).

The Church has grown now to cover the whole world. This gathering shall continue until the righteous are assembled in the congregations of the Saints in all nations of the world.

Joseph Smith said, "He who scattered Israel has promised to gather them; therefore inasmuch as you are to be instrumental in this great work"—read carefully—"He will endow you with power, wisdom, might, and intelligence, and every qualification necessary . . . until you can circumscribe the earth" (*History of the Church,* 4:129).

The Lord commanded, "Purify your hearts before me; and then go ye into all the world, and *preach my gospel* unto every creature who has not received it" (D&C 112:28; emphasis added). May we have the Spirit of the Almighty with us, that we may be gatherers in fulfillment of the prophecies. I invoke His blessings upon all of us in this great work, that His power can be felt, that the Holy Ghost will be our constant companion, and that we will go in peace to "preach [His] gospel."

22

THE WEAK AND THE SIMPLE OF THE CHURCH

In every general conference, we sustain the general officers of the Church in a solemn, sacred procedure. This common procedure occurs whenever leaders or teachers are called or released from office or whenever there is reorganization in a stake or a ward or a quorum or in the auxiliaries (see D&C 124:123, 144; see also D&C 20:65–67; 26:2). It is unique to The Church of Jesus Christ of Latter-day Saints.

We always know who is called to lead or to teach and have the opportunity to sustain or to oppose the action. It did not come as an invention of man but was set out in the revelations: "It shall not be given to any one to go forth to preach my gospel, or to build up my church, except he be ordained by some one who has authority, and *it is known to the church* that he has authority and has been regularly ordained by the heads of the church" (D&C 42:11; emphasis added). In this way, the Church is protected from any imposter who would take over a quorum, a ward, a stake, or the Church.

From an address given at general conference, October 6, 2007; see *Ensign,* Nov. 2007, 6–9.

There is another principle unique to the Lord's Church. All positions to teach and to lead are filled by members of the Church. This too has been set forth in the scriptures. One verse in the Doctrine and Covenants established the order of leadership in the Church for all time. It was unprecedented, certainly not the custom of Christian churches then or now:

"Wherefore, I the Lord, knowing the calamity which should come upon the inhabitants of the earth, called upon my servant Joseph Smith, Jun., and spake unto him from heaven, and gave him commandments; . . .

"The weak things of the world shall come forth and break down the mighty and strong ones, . . .

" . . . That every man might speak in the name of God the Lord, even the Savior of the world;

"That faith also might increase in the earth;

"That mine everlasting covenant might be established;

"That the fulness of my gospel might be proclaimed by the weak and the simple unto the ends of the world, and before kings and rulers.

"Behold, I am God and have spoken it; these commandments are of me, and were given unto my servants in their weakness, after the manner of their language, that they might come to understanding" (D&C 1:17, 19–24).

I am deeply grateful for those scriptures, which explain that the Lord will use the "weak things of the world."

Each member is responsible to accept the call to serve.

President J. Reuben Clark Jr. said: "In the service of the Lord, it is not where you serve but how. In the Church of Jesus Christ of Latter-day Saints, one takes the place to which one is duly called, which place one neither seeks nor declines" (in Conference Report, Apr. 1951, 154). The Church has no professional clergy. The call to leadership positions worldwide is drawn from the congregation. We have no seminaries for the training of professional leaders.

Everything that is done in the Church—the leading, the teaching, the calling, the ordaining, the praying, the singing, the preparation of the sacrament, the counseling, and everything else—is done by ordinary members, the "weak things of the world."

We see in the Christian churches their struggle to fill the need for clergy. We do not have that problem. Once the gospel is preached and the Church is organized, there is an inexhaustible supply of faithful brothers and sisters who have that testimony and are willing to answer the call to serve. They commit themselves to the work of the Lord and live the standards required of them.

Members have had the Holy Ghost conferred upon them after their baptism (see D&C 33:15; 35:6). The Holy Ghost will teach and comfort them. They are then prepared to receive guidance, direction, and correction—whatever their positions or needs require (see John 14:26; D&C 50:14; 52:9; 75:10).

This principle sets the Church on a different course from all other Christian churches in the world. We find ourselves in the unusual position of having an endless supply of teachers and leaders, among every nation and kindred and tongue and people, all over the world. There is a unique equality among members. No one of us is to consider himself or herself of more value than another (see D&C 38:24–25). "God is no respecter of persons: but in every nation he that feareth him, and worketh righteousness, is accepted with him" (Acts 10:34–35; see also Romans 2:11; D&C 1:35; 38:16).

When I was a young man, I was a home teacher to a very old sister. She taught me from her life experience.

When she was a little girl, President Brigham Young came to Brigham City, a great event in the town named after him. To honor him, the Primary children, all dressed in white, were lined up along the road coming into town, each with a basket of flowers to spread before the carriage of the President of the Church.

Something displeased her. Instead of throwing her blossoms, she kicked a rock in front of the carriage, saying, "He ain't one bit better than my Grandpa Lovelund." That was overheard, and she was severely scolded.

I am very sure that President Brigham Young would have been the first to agree with little Janie Steed. He would not have considered himself to be worth more than Grandpa Lovelund or any other worthy member of the Church.

The Lord Himself was very plain: "And whosoever will be chief among you, let him be your servant" (Matthew 20:27). "The same is appointed to be the greatest, notwithstanding he is the least and the servant of all" (D&C 50:26).

Years ago when I first received an appointment that resulted in my picture being in the newspapers, one of my high school teachers, evidently quite astonished, was heard to say, "That just proves that you can't tell by looking at a frog how high he is going to jump!"

The image of that frog, sitting in the mud instead of jumping, illustrates how inadequate I have felt when facing the responsibilities that have come to me. These feelings fix it so that thereafter one can never feel superior to anyone, not anyone.

For a long time, something else puzzled me. In 1961 I was a thirty-seven-year-old seminary supervisor. My Church calling was as an assistant teacher in a class in the Lindon Ward.

To my great surprise, I was called to meet with President David O. McKay. He took both of my hands in his and called me to be one of the General Authorities, an Assistant to the Quorum of the Twelve Apostles.

A few days later, I came to Salt Lake City to meet with the First Presidency to be set apart as one of the General Authorities of the Church. This was the first time I had met with the First Presidency—President David O. McKay and his counselors, President Hugh B. Brown and President Henry D. Moyle.

President McKay explained that one of the responsibilities of an

Assistant to the Twelve was to stand with the Quorum of the Twelve Apostles as a special witness and to bear testimony that Jesus is the Christ. What he said next overwhelmed me: "Before we proceed to set you apart, I ask you to bear your testimony to us. We want to know if you have that witness."

I did the best I could. I bore my testimony the same as I might have in a fast and testimony meeting in my ward. To my surprise, the Brethren of the Presidency seemed pleased and proceeded to confer the office upon me.

That puzzled me greatly, for I had supposed that someone called to such an office would have an unusual, different, and greatly enlarged testimony and spiritual power.

It puzzled me for a long time until finally I could see that I already had what was required: an abiding testimony in my heart of the Restoration of the fulness of the gospel through the Prophet Joseph Smith, that we have a Heavenly Father, and that Jesus Christ is our Redeemer. I may not have known all about it, but I did have a testimony, and I was willing to learn.

I was perhaps no different from those spoken of in the Book of Mormon: "And whoso cometh unto me with a broken heart and a contrite spirit, him will I baptize with fire and with the Holy Ghost, even as the Lamanites, because of their faith in me at the time of their conversion, were baptized with fire and with the Holy Ghost, *and they knew it not*" (3 Nephi 9:20; emphasis added).

Over the years, I have come to see how powerfully important that simple testimony is. I have come to understand that our Heavenly Father is the Father of our spirits (see Numbers 16:22; Hebrews 12:9; D&C 93:29). He is a father with all the tender love of a father. Jesus said, "For the Father himself loveth you, because ye have loved me, and have believed that I came out from God" (John 16:27).

Some years ago, I was with President Marion G. Romney, meeting with mission presidents and their wives in Geneva, Switzerland. He told them that fifty years before, as a missionary boy in Australia, late one afternoon he had gone to a library to study. When he walked out, it was night. He looked up into the starry sky, and it happened. The Spirit touched him, and a certain witness was born in his soul.

He told those mission presidents that he did not know any more surely then as a member of the First Presidency that God the Father lives; that Jesus is the Christ, the Son of God, the Only Begotten of the Father; and that the fulness of the gospel had been restored than he did as a missionary boy fifty years before in Australia. He said that his testimony had changed in that it was much easier to get an answer from the Lord. The Lord's presence was nearer, and he knew the Lord much better than he had fifty years before.

There is the natural tendency to look at those who are sustained to presiding positions, to consider them to be higher and of more value in the Church or to their families than an ordinary member. Somehow we feel they are worth more to the Lord than are we. It just does not work that way!

It would be very disappointing to my wife and to me if we supposed any one of our children would think that we think we are of more worth to the family or to the Church than they are, or to think that one calling in the Church was esteemed over another or that any calling would be thought to be less important.

When one of our sons was sustained as ward mission leader, his wife told us how thrilled he was with the call. It fit the very heavy demands of his work. He had the missionary spirit and found good use for his Spanish, which he had kept polished from his missionary days. We also were very, very pleased at his call.

But what my son and his wife are doing with their little children transcends anything they could do in the Church or out. No service could be more important to the Lord than the devotion they give to one another and to their little children. And so it is with all our other children. The ultimate end of all activity in the Church centers in the home and the family.

As General Authorities of the Church, we are just the same as you are, and you are just the same as we are. You have the same access to the powers of revelation for your families and for your work and for your callings as we do.

It is also true that there is an order to things in the Church. When you are called to an office, you then receive revelation that belongs to that office that would not be given to others.

No member of the Church is esteemed by the Lord as more or less than any other. It just does not work that way! Remember, He is a father—our Father. The Lord is "no respecter of persons."

We are not worth more to the onrolling of the Lord's work than were Brother and Sister Toutai Paletu'a in Nuku'alofa, Tonga; or Brother and Sister Carlos Cifuentes in Santiago, Chile; or Brother and Sister Peter Dalebout in the Netherlands; or Brother and Sister Tatsui Sato of Japan; or hundreds of others I have met while traveling about the world. It just does not work that way.

And so the Church moves on. It is carried upon the shoulders of worthy members living ordinary lives among ordinary families, guided by the Holy Ghost and the Light of Christ, which is in them. I bear witness that the gospel is true and that the worth of souls—every soul—is great in the sight of God.

23

THE LEAST OF THESE

There is a message for Latter-day Saints in a seldom quoted revelation given to the Prophet Joseph Smith in 1838. "I remember my servant Oliver Granger; behold, verily I say unto him that his name shall be had in sacred remembrance from generation to generation, forever and ever, saith the Lord" (D&C 117:12).

Oliver Granger was a very ordinary man. He was mostly blind, having "lost his sight by cold and exposure" (Joseph Smith, *History of The Church of Jesus Christ of Latter-day Saints,* 7 vols. [1932–1951], 4:408). The First Presidency described him as "a man of the most strict integrity and moral virtue; and in fine, to be a man of God" (ibid., 3:350).

When the Saints were driven from Kirtland, Ohio, in a scene that would be repeated in Independence, Far West, and Nauvoo, Oliver was left behind to sell their properties for what little he could. There

From an address given at general conference, October 3, 2004; see *Ensign,* Nov. 2004, 86–88.

was not much chance that he could succeed. And, really, he did not succeed!

But the Lord said, "Let him contend earnestly for the redemption of the First Presidency of my Church, saith the Lord; and when he falls he shall rise again, for his sacrifice shall be more sacred unto me than his increase, saith the Lord" (D&C 117:13).

What did Oliver Granger do that his name should be held in sacred remembrance? Nothing much, really. It was not so much what he did as what he was.

When we honor Oliver, much, perhaps even most of the honor should go to Lydia Dibble Granger, his wife.

Oliver and Lydia finally left Kirtland to join the Saints in Far West, Missouri. They had gone but a few miles from Kirtland when they were turned back by a mob. Only later did they join the Saints at Nauvoo.

Oliver died at age forty-seven, leaving Lydia to look after their children.

The Lord did not expect Oliver to be perfect, perhaps not even to succeed. "When he falls he shall rise again, for his sacrifice shall be more sacred unto me than his increase, saith the Lord" (D&C 117:13).

We cannot always expect to succeed, but we should try the best we can. "For I, the Lord, will judge all men according to their works, according to the desire of their hearts" (D&C 137:9).

The Lord said to the Church:

"When I give a commandment to any of the sons of men to do a work unto my name, and those sons of men go with all their might and with all they have to perform that work, and cease not their diligence, and their enemies come upon them and hinder them from performing that work, behold, it behooveth me to require that work no more at the hands of those sons of men, but to accept of their offerings. . . .

" . . . This I make an example unto you, for your consolation concerning all those who have been commanded to do a work and have been hindered by the hands of their enemies, and by oppression, saith the Lord your God" (D&C 124:49, 53; see also Mosiah 4:27).

The few in Kirtland are now millions of ordinary Latter-day Saints across the world. They speak a multitude of languages but unite in faith and understanding through the language of the Spirit.

These faithful members make and keep their covenants and strive to be worthy to enter the temple. They believe the prophecies and sustain the ward and branch leaders.

Like Oliver, they sustain the First Presidency and the Quorum of the Twelve Apostles and accept what the Lord said: "If my people will hearken unto my voice, and unto the voice of [these men] whom I have appointed to lead my people, behold, verily I say unto you, they shall not be moved out of their place" (D&C 124:45).

Now another generation of youth comes forward. We see a strength in them beyond what we have seen before. Drinking and drugs and moral mischief are not a part of their lives. They band together in study of the gospel, in socials, and in service.

They are not perfect. Not yet. They are doing the best they can, and they are stronger than the generations that came before.

As the Lord told Oliver Granger, "When [they fall they] shall rise again, for [their] sacrifice shall be more sacred unto me than [their] increase" (D&C 117:13).

Some worry endlessly over missions that were missed, or marriages that did not turn out, or babies that did not arrive, or children that seem lost, or dreams unfulfilled, or because age limits what they can do. I do not think it pleases the Lord when we worry because we think we never do enough or that what we do is never good enough.

Some needlessly carry a heavy burden of guilt which could be removed through confession and repentance.

The Lord did not say of Oliver, "*[If]* he falls," but "*When* he falls he shall rise again" (D&C 117:13; emphasis added).

Some years ago in the Philippines we arrived early for a conference.

Sitting on the curb were a father and mother and four small children dressed in their Sunday best. They had come several hours on a bus and were having the first meal of the day. Each of them was eating a cob of cold, boiled corn. The cost of the bus to Manila probably came out of their food budget.

As I watched that family, my heart overflowed with emotion. *There* is the Church. *There* is the power. *There* is the future. As with families in many lands, they pay their tithing, sustain their leaders, and do their best to serve.

For more than forty years, my wife and I have traveled over the earth. We know members of the Church in perhaps a hundred countries. We have felt the power in their simple faith. Their individual testimonies and their sacrifice have had a profound effect on us.

I do not like to receive honors. Compliments always bother me, because the great work of moving the gospel forward has in the past, does now, and will in the future depend upon ordinary members.

My wife and I do not expect reward for ourselves greater than will come to our own children or to our parents. We do not press nor do we really want our children to set great prominence and visibility in the world or even in the Church as their goal in life. That has so very little to do with the worth of the soul. They will fulfill our dreams if they live the gospel and raise their children in faith.

Like John, "[We] have no greater joy than to hear that [our] children walk in truth" (3 John 1:4).

Some years ago, as president of the New England Mission, I left Fredericton, New Brunswick. It was forty degrees below zero. As the plane taxied away from that small terminal, I saw two young elders standing outside, waving good-bye. I thought, "Foolish boys. Why do they not go inside where it's warm?"

Suddenly there came over me a powerful prompting, a revelation: There in these two ordinary young missionaries stands the priesthood of Almighty God. I leaned back, content to leave the missionary work for that entire province of Canada in their hands. It was a lesson I have never forgotten.

Elder William Walker of the Seventy and I once held a zone conference in Naha for forty-four missionaries on the island of Okinawa. President Mills of the Japan Fukuoka Mission was prevented from attending by an approaching ferocious typhoon. The young zone leaders conducted that meeting with as much inspiration and dignity as their mission president might have done. We left the next morning in gale-force winds, content to leave the missionaries in their care.

The calamities that the Lord foresaw now come upon an unrepentant world. At once, generation after generation of youth come forward. They are given in marriage. They keep the covenants made in the house of the Lord. They have children and do not let society set limits upon family life.

Today we fulfill the prophecy "that [Oliver Granger's] name shall be had in sacred remembrance from generation to generation, forever and ever" (D&C 117:12). He was not a great man in terms of the world. Nevertheless, the Lord said, "Let no man despise my servant Oliver Granger, but let the blessings . . . be on him forever and ever" (D&C 117:15).

Let no one underestimate the power of faith in the ordinary Latter-day Saints. Remember the Lord said, "Inasmuch as ye have done it unto one of the least of these my brethren, ye have done it unto me" (Matthew 25:40).

He promised that "the Holy Ghost shall be [their] constant companion, and [their] scepter an unchanging scepter of righteousness and truth; and [their] dominion shall be an everlasting dominion, and without compulsory means it shall flow unto [them] forever and ever" (D&C 121:46).

Nothing! No power can stop the progress of the Lord's work.

"How long can rolling waters remain impure? What power shall stay the heavens? As well might man stretch forth his puny arm to stop the Missouri river in its decreed course, or to turn it up stream, as to hinder the Almighty from pouring down knowledge from heaven upon the heads of the Latter-day Saints" (D&C 121:33).

Of this I bear an apostolic witness.

24

THESE THINGS I KNOW

In 1992, having served nine years as an Assistant to the Twelve and twenty-two years as a member of the Twelve, I reached the age of sixty-eight. I felt impressed to start what I called an "Unfinished Composition." The first part of that work goes like this:

> *I had a thought the other night,*
> *A thought profound and deep.*
> *It came when I was too worn down,*
> *Too tired to go to sleep.*
>
> *I'd had a very busy day*
> *And pondered on my fate.*
> *The thought was this:*
> *When I was young, I wasn't 68!*
>
> *I could walk without a limp;*
> *I had no shoulder pain.*

From an address given at general conference, April 6, 2013; see *Ensign*, May 2013, 6–8.

I could read a line through twice
And quote it back again.

I could work for endless hours
And hardly stop to breathe.
And things that now I cannot do
I mastered then with ease.

If I could now turn back the years,
If that were mine to choose,
I would not barter age for youth,
I'd have too much to lose.

I am quite content to move ahead,
To yield my youth, however grand.
The thing I'd lose if I went back
Is what I understand.

Ten years later, I decided to add a few more lines to that poem:

Ten years have flown to who knows where
And with them much of pain.
A metal hip erased my limp;
I walk quite straight again.

Another plate holds neck bones fast—
A wonderful creation!
It backed my polio away;
I've joined the stiff-necked generation.

The signs of aging can be seen.
Those things will not get better.
The only thing that grows in strength
With me is my forgetter.

You ask, "Do I remember you?"
Of course, you're much the same.

197

Now don't go getting all upset
If I can't recall your name.

I would agree I've learned some things
I did not want to know,
But age has brought those precious truths
That make the spirit grow.

Of all the blessings that have come,
The best thing in my life
Is the companionship and comfort
I get from my dear wife.

Our children all have married well,
With families of their own,
With children and grandchildren,
How soon they all have grown.

I have not changed my mind one bit
About regaining youth.
We're meant to age, for with it
Comes a knowledge of the truth.

You ask, "What will the future bring?
Just what will be my fate?"
I'll go along and not complain.
Ask when I'm 88!

And last year I added these lines:

And now you see I'm 88.
The years have flown so fast.
I walked, I limped, I held a cane,
And now I ride at last.

I take a nap now and again,
But priesthood power remains.

For all the physical things I lack
There are great spiritual gains.

I have traveled the world a million miles
And another million too.
And with the help of satellites,
My journeys are not through.

I now can say with all certainty
That I know and love the Lord.
I can testify with them of old
As I preach His holy word.

I know what He felt in Gethsemane
Is too much to comprehend.
I know He did it all for us;
We have no greater Friend.

I know that He will come anew
With power and in glory.
I know I will see Him once again
At the end of my life's story.

I'll kneel before His wounded feet;
I'll feel His Spirit glow.
My whispering, quivering voice will say,
"My Lord, my God, I know."

And I do know!

The back windows of our home overlook a small flower garden and the woods which border a small stream. One wall of the house borders on the garden and is thickly covered with English ivy. Most years this ivy has been the nesting place for house finches. The nests in the vines are safe from foxes and raccoons and cats that are about.

One day there was a great commotion in the ivy. Desperate cries of distress came as eight or ten finches from the surrounding woods came to join in this cry of alarm. I soon saw the source of the commotion. A snake had slid partway down out of the ivy and hung in front of the window just long enough for me to pull it out. The middle part of the snake's body had two bulges—clear evidence convicting it of taking two fledglings from the nest. Not in the fifty years we had lived in our home had we seen anything like that. It was a once-in-a-lifetime experience—or so we thought.

A few days later there was another commotion, this time in the vines covering our dog run. We heard the same cries of alarm, the gathering of the neighborhood finches. We knew what the predator was. A grandson climbed onto the run and pulled out another snake that was still holding on tightly to the mother bird it had caught in the nest and killed.

I said to myself, "What is going on? Is the Garden of Eden being invaded again?"

There came into my mind the warnings spoken by the prophets. We will not always be safe from the adversary's influence, even within our own homes. We need to protect our nestlings.

We live in a very dangerous world that threatens those things that are most spiritual. The family, the fundamental organization in time and eternity, is under attack from forces seen and unseen. The adversary is about. His objective is to cause injury. If he can weaken and destroy the family, he will have succeeded.

Latter-day Saints recognize the transcendent importance of the family and strive to live in such a way that the adversary cannot steal into our homes. We find safety and security for ourselves and our children in honoring the covenants we have made and living up to the ordinary acts of obedience required of the followers of Christ.

Isaiah said, "The work of righteousness shall be peace; and the effect of righteousness quietness and assurance for ever" (Isaiah 32:17).

That peace is also promised in the revelations in which the Lord declares, "If ye are prepared ye shall not fear" (D&C 38:30).

The consummate power of the priesthood has been given to protect the home and its inhabitants. The father has the authority and responsibility to teach his children and to bless and to provide for them the ordinances of the gospel and every other priesthood protection necessary. He is to demonstrate love and fidelity and honor to the mother so that their children can see that love.

I have come to know that faith is a real power, not just an expression of belief. There are few things more powerful than the faithful prayers of a righteous mother.

Teach yourself and teach your families about the gift of the Holy Ghost and the Atonement of Jesus Christ. You will do no greater eternal work than within the walls of your own home.

We know that we are spirit children of heavenly parents, here on earth to receive our mortal bodies and to be tested. We who have mortal bodies have the power over the beings who do not (see *Teachings of Presidents of the Church: Joseph Smith* [2007], 211). We are free to choose what we will and to pick and choose our acts, but we are not free to choose the consequences. They come as they will come.

Agency is defined in the scriptures as "moral agency," which means that we can choose between good and evil. The adversary seeks to tempt us to misuse our moral agency.

The scriptures teach us "that every man may act in doctrine and principle pertaining to futurity, according to the moral agency which I have given unto him, that every man may be accountable for his own sins in the day of judgment" (D&C 101:78).

Alma taught that "the Lord cannot look upon sin with the least degree of allowance" (Alma 45:16). In order to understand this, we must separate the sin from the sinner.

For example, when they brought before the Savior a woman taken in adultery, obviously guilty, He dismissed the case with five words: "Go, and sin no more" (John 8:11). That is the spirit of His ministry.

Tolerance is a virtue, but like all virtues, when exaggerated, it transforms itself into a vice. We need to be careful of the "tolerance trap" so that we are not swallowed up in it. The permissiveness afforded by the weakening of the laws of the land to tolerate legalized acts of immorality does not reduce the serious spiritual consequence that is the result of the violation of God's law of chastity.

All are born with the Light of Christ, a guiding influence which permits each person to recognize right from wrong. What we do with that light and how we respond to those promptings to live righteously is part of the test of mortality.

"For behold, the Spirit of Christ is given to every man, that he may know good from evil; wherefore, I show unto you the way to judge; for every thing which inviteth to do good, and to persuade to believe in Christ, is sent forth by the power and gift of Christ; wherefore ye may know with a perfect knowledge it is of God" (Moroni 7:16).

Each of us must stay in condition to respond to inspiration and the promptings of the Holy Ghost. The Lord has a way of pouring pure intelligence into our minds to prompt us, to guide us, to teach us, and to warn us. Each son or daughter of God can know the things they need to know instantly. Learn to receive and act on inspiration and revelation.

Of all that I have read and taught and learned, the one most precious and sacred truth that I have to offer is my special witness of Jesus Christ. He lives. I know He lives. I am His witness. And of Him I can testify. He is our Savior, our Redeemer. Of this I am certain.

INDEX

Death, women brought back from, 175–76
de Jager, Jacob, 80
Disabled children, 103
Discernment, Apostles possess gift of, 31
Disease, 141–42
Dispensation of the fulness of times, 19, 153–54
Diversity, 161
Divine nature, 111, 113–14
Doctrine and Covenants, 168
Drug abuse, 55

Education, 57
Elder: as title, 7; rights of, 8
Electricity, 35–36
Elias, 172
Elijah, 173
Endowment, 73
Ensign Peak, 149
Eve, 86
Exceptions, 16, 63, 109
Excommunication, 14–15

Fairbanks, John, 72
Family: priesthood and, 21–22, 50; Satan attacks, 25, 117; responsibilities in, 64–65; of Adam and Eve, 86; importance of maintaining, 90; in Church, 90–91, 94–99, 121–22; activities and schedule of, 96, 97–98, 123–24; tolerance and threats to, 114–15; eternal nature of, 124, 158; as center of plan of salvation, 126; temple work centered in, 180; protecting, 200–201. *See also*

"Family: A Proclamation to the World, The"; Home(s)
"Family: A Proclamation to the World, The": creation and standards of, 87; doctrine regarding premortal existence in, 88–89; parental duties enumerated in, 89–90; warning in, 90
Far West, Missouri, 173
Fathers: to preside in home, 21–22; blessings and ordinations performed by, 22–23; responsibilities of, 25, 50, 90, 201. *See also* Parents
Father's blessing, for soldier, 22–23
Fear, of future, 139–45, 151
Finches, 199–200
First Presidency: establishment of, 28–29; as prophets, seers, and revelators, 29; unity of Twelve Apostles and, 32–33, 130; ages of, 136; issues "A Proclamation of the First Presidency of the Church to the Saints Scattered Abroad," 176–77
First Vision, 85, 159
Fox Islands, 174–76
Friends, 105–6
Funeral, for child, 119–20
Future, fear of, 139–45, 151

Gathering of Saints, 172–82
Gender, 55, 88
Gideon, 18–19
God: and oath and covenant of priesthood, 9; trust of, for His children, 49, 50; as Heavenly Father, 85, 187; love of, 100;

and women in, 117–18; family as
center of, 126
Polio, 54
Population, and birthrate, 116, 134
Pornography, 55, 159
Power of godliness, 16–17
Power of priesthood, 18–26, 35–37,
42–44, 52–53
Practical knowledge, 57
Prayer, 159
Premortal existence, 88–89, 125
Priesthood authority: conferral of,
10; limits to, 10–11; ordination
and, 13; distribution of, 21; versus
power, 25; of Aaronic Priesthood,
39–42, 52–53; apostasy and, 157;
restoration of, 157
Priesthood blessing(s): for soldier,
22–23; for healing, 45–46. *See also*
Patriarchal blessings
Priesthood government, 3–4, 169–70
Priesthood keys. *See* Keys of the
priesthood
Priest: minimum age for ordination
as, 11; responsibilities of, 40
"Proclamation of the First Presidency
of the Church to the Saints
Scattered Abroad, A," 176–77
Procreation, 114, 117, 120, 126,
150, 158–59
Prophets, Apostles as, 29
Provident living, 112

Quorums, 8–9, 41

Record keeping, 16
Refuge, 153, 154
Relief Society, 60–67, 109, 134

Repentance, through Atonement, 56,
121, 128–29
Restoration: Twelve Apostles and,
28–29; order of, 46–49, 157;
and turning hearts of children to
fathers, 134–35
Revelation(s): on priesthood
government, 4; Church guided
by, 47–48, 86; publication of,
157–58, 165; continuing, 168–69;
receiving and acting on, 202. *See
also* Holy Ghost
Revelators, Apostles as, 29
Richards, LeGrand, 40, 72
Richards, Willard, 149–50
Rigdon, Sidney, 95
Romney, Ida, 176
Romney, Marion G., 176, 178,
187–88

Sacrament, 37–38, 56
Sacrifice, 38
Salt Lake Temple: dedication of,
68–69; construction of, 70–72;
visitations to, 72
Salt Lake Valley: settlement of, 149–
50; gathering in, 176–78
Salvation, 50–51, 144–45. *See also*
Baptism for the dead
Satan: attacks home and family, 25,
117, 200; resisting, 56; influence
of, 125; tactics of, 158–60
Schooling, 57
Scriptures: knowledge of, 165; LDS
edition of, 166, 167–69; gathering
as recurring theme of, 181
Seers, Apostles as, 29
Seminary graduation, 105